Rock as Gloss

Rock as Gloss

Mark Goodwin

Longbarrow Press

Published in 2019 by
Longbarrow Press
76 Holme Lane
Sheffield
S6 4JW

www.longbarrowpress.com

Printed by T.J. International Ltd,
Padstow, Cornwall

Poems and fiction in this collection, or versions of, have
been previously published (or accepted for publication)
by the following, to whose editors I am grateful:
*Alpinist; Cornwall – Chair Ladder, the South Coast, and
the Lizard, The Climbers' Club Guides; The Climbers' Club
Journal; Froggatt to Black Rocks, British Mountaineering
Council; Gull; Kootenay Mountain Culture Magazine;
The Journal of Wild Culture; Llanberis Slate, Ground Up;
the Longbarrow Press blog; The New Writer; Poetry Scotland;
Stanage – The Definitive Guide, British Mountaineering
Council; Staple (1990s); Tears in the Fence; Texts' Bones.*

ISBN 978-1-906175-36-8

First edition

Legend

Compass I

Compass II

Compass IV

for Nick, and his passion for words

and for Arthur, who taught me to climb

the gritstone is constantly settling
if you doubt grit settling

you do not know
your own settling

.

art is a dot
you add to day by day
a right line piled
high

.

Meanings that will not part from the rock.

.

The climbers. They. They and their hills.

Compass I

a ripped poet's coil
of snake saying

changed

Rock Climbing for Novices

To begin   notice,

with a tinge of fantastic, cracks in pavements,
gaps between bricks. Uneven-natured surfaces. Ignore,

at the outset, outdoors-sports shops
that sell the greatly-varied, bright ways of knowing
the ropes.

▲

All journeys have narrators. Shapes, fragrances, textures
(things that first spored words) pronounce
silent dialects of signposts. Take this crack, close
                    its edges
over your eyes; give yourself rhyolite eyelids. Push

your mind's nose into mineral-cool zing tinged
with moist fluffs of dead plant & insect; heavy
with potential weight of life. Open
            your eyes;
feel them in your sockets smooth as raindrops. Look

with water. The crack
is habitat of surprise. Ferns
stick out frond-tongues at intrusion: imp

-ertinent little girls of greenery; harmless but
so powerfully intimidating. Forget

tilts of the odyssey above; you must
navigate massive intricacies – a mass
of stimuli jumbling in an area of inches
(or if it's your preference – centimetres). Yet remember

you can't measure any of this. As air drips
as moss-slime, as moss-slime swirls
as wind, so this
entire continent of cliff shrinks
to meet endless expanses of slabs that facet
minute granules. How this crack

contains a sensation of pressed flesh. Let,
if you're seeing insides of rhyolite eyelids,

sun's light shine through rock.

▲

Now, if you must, go to the shop.

1996 (slight editing 2016)

A Climber is Dialling Stone

from *Museum of The Stanage-ophone*

the climber is dialling the stone
his fingers electrical contacts

the operator is very old   is very patient   the operator is Time

a climber is trying to get through
but the stone holds for the moment are engaged
the climber is dialling the stone

     sorry, you have dialled incorrectly, please try again

dialling dialling dialling   fingerprints tapping   finger
prints rubbing finger   prints ripping

     can you hold please

see how he is an ear
the whole ear of a self pressed
against this ancient receiver   the curly flex
of Stanage Edge's length ready

to transmit his question

along receding wires of desire   our climber is dialling
dialling   dialling   dialling

hear how his skin sees
something   beneath
rock's   surface

feel how grit rasps   then suddenly

stone-hello stone-hello stone-hello welcome

you are through

to the Stanage-ophone
to Grittish Tellestone
to the Tell-Stone of Motion

through to

rock's survival hotline

now

the conversation begins

2003 (slight editing 2016)

a climb's holds hold
a time of

skin flesh blood
bone flowing pattern

rock likens no self
to rock as sky's

air shapes lungs

20 KM²

fingers on Froggatt grit grip   cling
to Stoke Flat's lip   a climber

       presses

her nose to grainy stone   focuses
on one vast square inch   the Derwent

       slips

sparks between trees   stitches
a shine to the valley bottom   a shepherd

mesmerised by a rabbit fixed
by a weasel's kill-glare

       stands

like a stone   inscribed   in a Froggatt cottage
a girl's hand on a cat's sleek black coat is

       lit

by aeon-travelling light slanting
in through glass   a beech leaf

in Bee Wood   trembles
in breeze as a wasp's silhouette

       clings

to that leaf's backlit skin   beyond
and above the valley   Big Moor

       goes

on hanging its still
& mottled

                    dream

i have in
my hands a

map of
water as

i turn by
degrees to

find

my or a way

at all drop
lets of

location drip

from my
fingers in

to rivu   lets
losing me

Bored as a Boy on a Beach

bored on a beach
with no rocks big enough

I let sand
trickle out from between
                    my teeth

no good crag
just little and

brittle boulders of rotten rock
                    to play on

each sequence of moves changed
    as I moved over them – choss

that I had to abandon
    so maddened I ate

sand

or at least filled
my mouth with it un

til I yawned and
    gaped to let

the dry crystal rock-bits seep
                    out over my lower

lip like excitement dying

then in my bland mind I made
    a man a mere millimetre tall

and let him loose into
a world of oversized adventure

blocks that had had tops
    only as high as my
               chin

became hundreds
of times the length of anything
            in Yosemite

my millimetre man
with his man-size millimetre ego

and id

first made the approach march across
vast shifting moraines of giant molecules
          made solely of silica

then at last at the crag's base
        he'd begin

up Mount Impossible

following a stonking crack-line through
        dark glorious roofs and

then across sumptuous
prairies of blank gleaming
slabs he danced and pushed

on and
ever upwards

yet disappointment would seep
        back into my mouth like

slowly sicking sand backwards

for once high enough
    and free of his old
            horizon he'd

see the sea

and at its edge

massive girls in massive
    scant bikinis moving

with the strange distant grace
            of giraffes

stag in   a slot
bet   wixt bens

lone silhou   ette letter from
land's unwri   tten

alph   abet

Metaphysical Mountaineer
With Ropes of Rock and Bells of Air – S.T.C.

In cuts fells' dirt tingles. Skinned
        knuckles buzz
crags' graceless caresses. High cold ridges to

       beyond bridge

flesh to thunder's electrics – navigated
by old youth's starlight eyes. Raw eyelids flicker

       storm. Bone clangs

stone-dense agonies. Meat and spirit commune
like tongues of cloud-light lick
Lakeland ground. Ornate pains tinkle;

       clatter across rough
       sheets of scree; spill

flocks of stone starlings; force
liquid wheels to polish

       chasms; make

ancestral prayers slippery. Broken spectres grope
over clouds' heaving desires. Lust's whittled

sublime by wind's disciplines. Mists' doubts refract

rainbows. Sun's rolling lyric glows;
      falls;
           sows
autumn's leaves with voices' seeds; lights
spent webs of veins until dark bleeds.

      Moon drips

silvery milk into ghylls; glints
photons of fluttering doves across
open-pupil tarns. Sinking

      feelings rise.

1999 (original draft)

as a climber clings
to a rippled quartzite wall
gulls surf salt's updraughts

                                    as to gulls

        clings wall up   draughts

                            climber-rippled surf

        sore quartzite nods

                            three in thrift

fingers pocket un

    knowingly whilst hooked

                three sore fingers   hooked
                in a quartzite pocket   whilst
                thrift nods un   knowingly

Climber

hard as light
broken in ice

his hands rock-ragged
he ties

cold ropes
to an old

man's mind

crags of gold
hold a home's

wandering lines

why tie in
to regrets

& wishes?

why does stone shine
like gold yet home

not hold fast?

he replies
with a smile like mist

blurring a lochan

and he shrugs
like wind-hardened

snows suddenly sliding

into a glen

along an arête
nuthatch-neat a boy scampers

as sea-sh   ine s   urges

A seagull's shadow
slides across snappy Lizard
stone. A climber aches.

A Ghost Jokes

Menlove Edwards peels

off a pair of dainty sticky
-rubber shoes – reveals

leather boots nailed
scuffed-&-gleaming. Smiles

with terrifying kindness, then tears
a bright hi-tech-textile jacket

        off his chest. And there

   he is

in a woollen blazer all
ripped-&-stitched. He plays

a poet's pipe to a pretty
coil of kernmantle making

it snake
        away hawser-laid. He laughs

saying: 'Ah, nothing has
changed.' And you can see

   he is

happy-&-sad for that

first drafted: 1997

the   leaf stuck to my boot
the   raven on the cairn

a   drystone wall's etch across snow
      reflected in two

      parts of a tarn

a book in
a bothy in a

glen among
silent bens in

that book
a poem a

bout a
bothy by

a burn
reading its

bed
of pe

                bbles

Munro by Gone

One moment bright sunshine. Blasts of bright golds & silvers (never sure which) from snow along the ridge. Now down amongst grey wet breath. One moment up amongst blue air with soft clouds tangling with eyebrows & beard, wanting ... wanting to step up above the summit, step out along slick silence of sky, smooth of forever. Crampons crunching on crystallised skin, skin of gods & goddesses laid down through an archaeology of weather. Amongst scree & boulders two ptarmigan in winter plumage pretend very well, O how well they believe they can be quartz, but I am so proud of myself for spotting their feathers. Now a valley's mouth closes over one self amongst many ... closes into a gut of mythology, moraines, bone-frame birches, deep loss-hot lochans with cold grey membranes. All that's left of the bothy are walls. Moss has clothed many of the stones – stones looking regal in plush emeralds. Gently vibrating drops of water sound like condensed trumpets now and so utterly concentrated flutes then. There is absolutely no hint of bagpipes. The young birch in the corner is coquettish as the breeze activates her. The purple mistiness of her twigs & the cream papery stripes of her skin remind a community not present of a song never made. Why can't I be on the mountain? The burn a few metres away did not ask that question, but a phrase of its racing water over stone codes will be heard that way. There is a woman, she has tartan cloth in her lap & a bright splinter held precisely between her index finger & thumb. The bothy is her heart she is pumped by. A boy's voice like scree sliding, yet also like breeze through grasses has her name wrapped up in itself: repeating vowels & consonants like melting & freezing at once in an instance: a boy's voice wallowing inside the sound ... My crampons look like traps, my ice-axe is a killer. I lay them down, my tools of travel, on a mossy stone, like a ritual – silly-Billy! My technical rucksack is from centuries up ahead.

The orange Gore-Tex of my jacket (which is made in China by an American outdoor clothing company) is as miraculous as a space-suit. Other planets are caught up in woollen galaxies. A woman woven from wool. Threads of flesh & twines of bone. The lochan just up the way is ready to drink the people, the people are transparent more & more each day. I will watch in amazement as my crampons seemed to soften then so often melt as if the stone they were resting on ... is very very hot. My ice axe went, it never comes again. The little bothy wears itself on the land like a wound, the soft open hole of home. There is the smell of ... The roof turned into a crow then just flapped away. Simple as that! That, that, that. I take off my hat. A complete circle slips from my skull. A complete round plan crowns the ground. The funnel of the wind has much fascination for my heat. On a little island in one of the lochans in the next corrie an aircraft engine (from a warplane) rests like a lost tooth; some way away a bent propeller pretends to be a sycamore key. The crumbling bothy invites the guests of weather in, then the home is raucous with elemental revellers. We've all seen the tumbleweed coming in off the desert, in the movies. A pale rider is dragging a frightened yet inquisitive birch tree into the barn made of snow clouds. I am wide awake, not dreaming, my ribcage is wide open, the red grass of my insides has sprouted, it is growing so well in the soil of reverie, a breeze makes my red grass swish. The glistening ridge of snow winks as the sky-grey rips open to blue then heals shut again. Stiff grey clouds, balls of wiry mist are falling from the lip of the corrie, rolling down the side of the burn. The grey wiremists have hooves. The bothy roof flapped away as flames. One book took four signatures & seven hundred or so souls to print. The oddest thing. My crampons are a gin-trap, a tiny mountain is caught between their teeth, the little mountain is struggling to be free, to get back with the wind, but its snow is turning black. Not sadness, exactly. Nothing exactly. My red grass is being eaten.

Wire wool, wiry mist clouds, hooves, flat chisel-teeth, eyes with slots where coins can be pushed. *Thin silly messages.* The woman working with wool dissolves her face with whispering her son's name. The musk of rutting stags & the scent of bread tangle in air to the death. Bright blasts. Gold & silver in the wet purse of a lochan. One moment. Yes, just.

a little shed
under

a big hill &
a mile

wide cloud

one

            window

                gl

            eams

foot   to gr   ound
hand   to grou   nd

head   to air

br   eath

brea   th

                        brea   the

faint cri   nkle
of clo   th on

li   mbs

Adeptitude @
The Plantation During
Hundreds-of-Thousands-of-Years-&-
A-December-Afternoon
for Paul

        and

        here where

        boulders hold

        matters

in no
one   ,

        s

        hands as

their geoevolution flashes
by by being by be

        ing

        still

                solidity

        has

        said these grey

        beech trees' shapes play

ing out
like

Stanage Edge
's cracks through

       pliable growth

       and

       here

       now as

sinking sun
fractures in

       mist now

now grit's
solidity is

       is

       is say

       ing says

       this

       person's forms his

want
ing to   ,

need
ing to

     fit

selves to
this

     this this

     grit

     ,

     s

     speed

Compass II

meaningless night's universe
the wind the stones   sea
her variant

Special Lighting, E2 5c †

One way or the other I dreamt
that I was in two parts. – M.E.

Can't remember the crag. Probably Wales, or some version-of. Thing is, I've learned everything's a version of something else. And people, humans, loved ones or strangers – they are just as changeable & ever-weathering as landscapes or frost-threatened rock routes, or historical accounts of sporting past-times. Times past. Time passes! In the end, at the last stance of the day, all people are really only versions of themselves or other people. Always versions. Route descriptions are just versions of someone's idea of a way up something. Oh yeh! How many times we've all been on a crag, all of us, and the route description seems to be the version of a climb we're not actually right-now climbing, thank you very much! I'm rambling – sorry, bad joke. Climbing! Take in! You taking this in?

Do you want to here & now the story? I bet, I just bet you do. But I bet also, just like the rest, when you hear it you won't believe it. Yes, I'm bonkers – as a cow-bell in a rurp-split. But buddy, the big twenty-four thousand pitch question's about you. Yes, you! Are you going to dismiss the whole ascent just for one moment of odd route description?

As far as I care, what I'm going to tell you – that I've told dozens already, from nurses to doctors, to mum & dad, and my wife – far as I care it really happened. And if it didn't – then far as I care for anything it really did anyway. That's what a lot of people don't get – just like climbing, it's all in the head. If you think that all-in-the-head isn't real then you really are off-route, in the mist and it's beginning to piss. Mental illness is contagious – if your partner loses it on the crux of some sandbag, or just at the kitchen sink, doesn't matter where, then for sure you'll be losing something of yourself as well.

My climbing partner, Vince, was a very good climber – steady, strong, bold, but not reckless. Solid E2 leader. Vince The Able & Invincible, I used to call him. Just a bit of a tosser when it came to women. But that's another story. Never mind, shame about his love life, but climbing with him was wonderful – some of the happiest days of my previous life. Anyway, we turn up at the base of that famous beautiful mountain crag ... only famous to yourself, but you know the one I mean. Soft, sunny September day. Smell of old leaves rising up through the woods far below. Golden sunlight drizzled into the grass, every blade crisp as if it'd been made in a jeweller's workshop. Vince's eyes, as always, keen on the crag, and the light dancing in the green of his irises – seemed as if he was making the crag happen by staring at it. The crag gleamed, warm & rough. You know the kind of day – just can't wait to feel the stone and be getting going.

Things start going wrong, for me at least, when I notice Vince is wearing a tweed jacket. Usually wears a Craig-Kit® soft-shell. And what the sandbag-bastard has he got on his feet? Big bloody dockers' boots, with nails. Who do you think you are, Vince? Looks me straight in the eye, no joking, and he says: Menlove Edwards. Great, get to go climbing with one of the 1930s legends, bloody great! Well no, it's not! I just want to go climbing with Vince. I like, or liked, I will like – can't remember the order of pitches here, sometimes the guidebook gets things arse-about-face, you know, the 4b pitch turns out to be the 5c one, just like finding out that your friend was crying not laughing, or worse the other way round, in the wrong order, wrong-wrong-wrong! Anyway, I always liked Vince's long chestnut-blond hair, it was kind of comforting to see it wavering in the breeze as he disposed of the crux like he was drawing a loved one's face with just thirteen quick perfect pen strokes. You see, Vince was an artist as well. Did I tell you? But now his hair has gone – neat 1930s short-back-&-sides. Now why was that? Why was a detail like that so very very bloody important? Just one slight bit of miss-info and the whole route becomes another route and you end up climbing something desperate & fab or you end up with a guidebook with no words & no topos just full of black daggers because, oh by-the-way, you died. Doornail. Bloody doornail! It wasn't my fault. Why did he decide to come dressed like that? And then the light changed as well. Went darker. Not cold & dim. Kind of warm dark. With freshly painted stage scenery, still damp. And special lighting. As if both of us in separate spotlights but moving up the cliff together. Connected. It's our show – me in one spotlight on belay, him in another spotlight way up the face. And the thin lines of our nylon bonds gleaming between us. And the audience – just the bloody sheep, the ravens, & the hills beyond. The rest of the world, or bloody wrong versions of it, can't & couldn't touch us. Thing I wanted to know, want to know – who or what the bastard-sandbag was shining those spotlights on us? Shining, shining right to the end of a climb. Who? Same bloody questions the owls ask. Who? Who?

Want to know what, what ... what will really make you ill? That'd be seeing someone you love just decide to check out early. Thank you Mister Landlord of The Crag, I will be checking out from Black Crag Inn early on in the climb. If you don't mind, let me just hand over this little wire, it's my last piece of gear, the one that would keep me from the jagged rocks below, and the hungry black mouth of the little llyn that wants to eat me up, but you take it, Crag Landlord, & this also, this little note to my climbing partner, you must get it to him, he's in room number two on the hanging stance ninety feet below, in his own spotlit pool, this very moment gazing up at us, you just make sure he gets this note and also ... And then there's a moist cracking sound as Vince, and I see him do this, he pushes his sandbagging hand through his ribs and rips out the throbbing bloody muscle that was his centre and plonks it into The Black-Crag-Lord's hand. Vince then shouts: 'I'm checking out!' Not: 'Take in!', no, couldn't shout that, he shouts: 'Checking out!'

Vince decks out.

Just one spotlight left on the face – me in the final act. The bloody curtains are stuck though. Just want to go home and have a hot bath. But the bloody stained curtains in this version of North Wales on the Dark Crag ... the curtains won't close and the show is going on. So, Vince is lying there smashed at the bottom, but still has the audacity to pretend he's Menlove Edwards. He's dead, but still banging on about how much better 1930s climbers are than 21st Century climbers simply on account of how technical clothing is a poor version of human skin and it's better to wear wool as that's closer to nature. He's yelling this loud as hell up the crag, and he's dead. You think *I'm* mad! Go on then, if you're so smart, with your newly printed guidebook, your lead ... you tell me a better version of who I am. Yes?

This next bit is what no one believes. I untied the ropes, and soloed up the pitch Vince-or-Menlove-or-whoever-he-was had just parted company from. Parted company. Parted company! Now I used to be a steady E1 leader, but there's me soloing E2 5c, and each handhold is soft & smooth as skin, sweaty skin in places, and yet I dance it like a Spaniard sad & glad all in one for his bull he's about to slay. And at the top of the pitch I find a rope made from hair. Same colour as Vince's hair – brown with golden threads, rich with the lucid season of September. Wasn't Vince's hair though, was just a version. That's how I got down – just slid down a rope of some bloke's hair. Do you know the one about Rapunzel? Kind o' like that but different characters, of course.

At the bottom Vince was a mess. And he wouldn't speak to me. After seventeen years together, on all sorts of climbs, from frozen water through grit, quartzite, limestone, slate & granite, and he just lies there pretending to be Menlove Edwards. Won't say a bloody word to me. Just as silent as if he was that faint face in

a dream I &
you & every

other bleedin' climber there
was or ever will

be dreams

Slackline & Tarn

The tarn is a narrow length of water cradled in a corridor between rocky knolls. The young woman is sitting cross-legged on a tussock at the southern end of this geological lane. She is staring at a thin red strip of nylon webbing that has been stretched from a craglet on the eastern side of the corridor to a craglet on the western side. The red strip of nylon is some twenty feet above the clear gleaming yet dark water, and its span across the gap runs to about ninety feet. The sky is empty blue but for a few fine fibres of cloud. There is a fresh westerly breeze, and a hum like a blown reed, and sometimes a soft buzz as rushing air vibrates the nylon line's edges.

Every now and again the young woman's black hair is moved gently by the breeze as it swirls in, and swirls out of the corridor. It is mid-morning, so she can feel the sun on her right cheek, and on her left cheek the cool off the water. She can also smell the watery-ness of the dark tarn as its gently glinting edges slosh its grassy banks. Fresh spring reeds poke up from the shallows. In this moment her blue eyes are fixed on the tarn's surface and the dark clarity of its depths – she is repeatedly changing her focus of vision from the silvered ripples & wobbling surface reflections to the hollow black below ... that the stirred surface in turns hides and reveals. And so in turns the tarn appears to her as an opaque shivering lid, then as a limpid mass with shafts of light slicing it ... and then deeper down the space blooms into a cavity of thickening darkness.

Suddenly a black shape shifts swiftly across the surface-ripples. It is a reflected raven. She looks into the sky a broad smile growing on her face as the raven tips itself upside down on the air then with a twizzle rights itself again its claws like little gleeful aerials. Now the raven *cronks*, and the rumble of its voice so delights the young woman that she laughs outloud. Hers is a laugh that has been at once pulled out of her by the power of another creature, and at the same time has been projected from far inside her body pushed by her mind. She tries her laugh again, and whilst watching this dark gymnast of the air, and enjoying its black flames of ruffling-feather, she listens for the brief echo of her laughter, as the soundwaves she makes bounce from stone and glide over water. The young woman is wise enough to know she cannot ever meet with a wild raven, and yet her laugh feels like some sign of kinship.

Now she thinks of the beautiful young man who set up the slackline, the man who stretched the thin line across the gap. At the moment he is out of sight, he is checking the slackline's anchor on the back of the western craglet. She is waiting for him to re-appear, for him to take his first step off the rocky edge onto the swaying thin red stripe of vibrating nylon above the dark clarity of the tarn. She thinks of his kind yet somehow evasive face, his strong mouth, his green eyes often cool yet sometimes agitated like a distracted child's, and his long blond hair, so often streaming in the wind, or gleaming in sunlight. And she can hear his voice in her memory, hear his so often shining *and* bewitching phrases that he himself never listens to.

Her mind now takes her back some hours ago ... and some miles away below the edge of the little plateau holding the narrow tarn ... just as the notes of the dawn chorus were beginning tweet by whistle to drop out of and jump from the dim-lit forms of dawn trees, they had sat together below a huge sprawling yew tree in the graveyard of the ruined church in the valley's mouth. She had watched the dawnlight glide through the yew's branches to grow its glow in his hair. And he had noticed an ancient stone cross, and at its base there seemed to be a carved face; a face dominated by, as he had put it, a gaping O of surprise. A gaping O of surprise. She had repeated his words to him, and as usual she had watched his face closely as she re-sang his voice back to him. For a second his eyes had looked into hers as if he had heard her heard himself quoted but then as usual he'd looked away. And as usual he'd said nothing about her picking up his words and holding them ... holding them in her mouth ... and then her turning them in the air as if they were jewels to catch and bounce the Sun's light just as that star, the Earth's closest star, crested the silhouette of the fell to their east.

Do you know why they call me Nark? he had said to her, and she had replied: Yes, of course. And even though he had told her many times by now, as in some playful ritual he told her yet again, and she, as always, listened carefully and lovingly, but also partly like a fox trying to catch sight of some small creature she had just smelled amongst the grasses. It is because once after what was my longest un-harnessed highline walk, across the Tagonachi Gap in Japan, the travel writer Seth Douglas had asked me: Do you agree, as many are now saying, that you are addicted, that this nylon line you step on is some kind of narcotic? And I, I don't know why, but I said to him: It is not the line, it is I that is the narcotic. And so Seth Douglas dubbed me Narcotic Chrisall, and in time my friends eroded my new name to 'Nark'. But enough of me. What about you? Why do they call you Echo? And to continue their playful ritual, to expand the set piece of their companionable drama she had, as always, replied: Why do they call you Echo? You Echo? Echo? And then, as ever, she followed that with her gleaming laughter. And next, as was their custom, she explained: Eccleshall, my second name of course, I've told you before, told you before, since primary school my friends have compressed Eccleshall to Echo. I'm sure, sure you know this. Know this. And then as was usual, and of habit, he replied: Well, Michelle, do you always pronounce the end of your last name as 'hall'? Have you ever considered trying saying it as 'shall'? I have not, but that is very clever! Can you Nark, tell me why you so often wear yellow? Is it to match your long golden locks? No, Echo my love, it is not. It is because Toshiro Stix, the great Japanese balancer & calligraphist, after my passing over the Tagonachi Gap, he presented to me a gorgeous yellow silk kimono, appliquéd with tiny black petals. And, Echo, this is what he said to me: Adam Chrisall ~san, it is not common to Japanese mythology, but I know the colour yellow is the colour of passing from one dream to the next, and you, Adam Chrisall ~san my friend, are a great Dream Walker. And then, as always, in reply Echo sang: A great dream walker. Dream walker. Walker. And she gave him yet again that which she knew he loved the feel of in his ear, she gave her voice. And then her laughter was like sunlight entwined with bubbling water ... but with a difference, for this time it had mixed in with the growing notes of the valley's dawn chorus ...

Splosh. A stone splits the tarn's surface. The crisp wet sound jolts her to the present. And then she hears Nark's voice. Hokay, Echo, set the camera going. She shouts back: Hokay Echo! And as she yells *Echo* again, she recalls glimpsing just for a split second and just from a fraction-of-a-second ago the chucked pebble wobbling its fall through the tarn's light before it entered the dark. Now she presses the bright sharp-blue flashing LED button on the silvery cube perched on its three silvery legs. And she shouts again: Camera going. Going!

She gazes at the craggy top of the western edge of the corridor, just where the red nylon line meets it. The sky behind the rocks & the red strip is deep blue. She is waiting for Nark's shape to appear. And then he is there, at the edge. He is wearing the yellow kimono, its silk shimmers in the mid-morning light. He is barefoot, and he takes the first step onto the red nylon. Suddenly she feels fear, even though this line is short and only twenty feet above water, even though this walk is just for pleasure and holds no challenge for Nark ... she suddenly feels a pang, as if an icicle had just this moment been carefully pushed under her ribcage, the pain sharp cold slowly melting away.

Gently and smoothly Nark moves out step by slow step across the red slackline. He will do no stunts nor tricks. No backflips or astounding balances. No running or hopping. He has told her that all he will do today is simply but very slowly walk across the narrow tarn in his yellow kimono, and have the silvery cube film it. And enjoy her watching him. And enjoy angling his body and the kimono to the breeze to feel the buoyancy of flying and at the same time know the firm line's sway and bounce under each barefoot step and enjoy the touch of the faint coiling strands of his planet's gravity on his fingertips as his arms divine a particular space & place … and enjoy the colours and the light and the textures of Anglo upland its grasses heather & rocks its clear air and the gleaming water and the shimmer of the water and the spangles of its reflected light wriggling over the yellow hissing silk of the kimono given him.

And there Nark is, in the middle of the red line. Blue sky behind. His yellow kimono blazing … the rustle of the fabric mixing in with the breeze's buzz as it rubs the red nylon's edges. His sleek yellow figure is reflected on the dark surface of water below him. The reflected yellow sheen wavers like a yolk just flopped from a cracked egg and it wobbles and then fractures and disappears amongst a silvery writhing wire-work of ripples as the breeze suddenly coils into the corridor to skitter across the dark tarn's pliant skin. And the young woman is watching so very very closely. She can smell the dissolved minerals in the water: a foil of scent lifted off the surface sprayed through the air. Suddenly she thinks how perfect the film would be if the black ragged raven would now appear again and twirl its black flames … now …

… now a watery crash of a body much larger than a mere chucked pebble breaks the narrow tarn's surface and sets it flowing with expanding circles of wavelets. And the young man balancing in the yellow kimono is gone. The young man in the yellow kimono is gone. He is gone. The red line vibrates empty in the air. The black yet clear water of the tarn slowly settles. Its ripples subside. The young woman stares at the surface sheen. Then past the surface through the limpid cool. Down she stares into the black closet beyond the light. Now yet another coil of air wrinkles the water impenetrable. She stares. Stares at the surface. She. At the surface. She stares ...

... years dissolve and go by ... storms scurry across her ... centuries, as people far away from her measure them, come and go ... airless sunlight falls like sheets of steel ... moonless & moonlit nights alike repeatedly form around her and repeatedly disappear ... and still the young woman sits cross-legged on the shore of the narrow tarn ... the grass & heather withered away scores of decades ago ... the silvery cube & its tripod is now a few mangled components smudged with corrosion ... she sits on grit amongst naked rocks, and the narrow tarn is now very low down in the bottom of its deep rocky slot ... but still she sits through all this ... her clothes have blown away from her long ago ... and still she is not rotting flesh, and she is not whitened bones ... she sits watching and listening and she is keenly alive ... the sun's rays grow stronger ... slowly the tarn's water dries ... she will wait, patiently in the desert ... every now and again she goes to the very edge of the narrow slot with the gleam in the bottom of it and she throws her shout and waits as her yell falls down towards the remaining water towards the water the water water ... she keeps her vigil ... she listens ... she keeps her gaze glowing ... how she hopes one day to at least just glimpse his bones wrapped in the silk of his yellow chrysalis ... she will not give ... she will ... she will not ... not give in ... give in ... in ...

Cracked Gabbro

The air is part of the mountain, which does not
come to an end with its rock & its soil.
                                    – Nan Shepherd

B   ut the most striking pre   sence in the room is above the fire   place: expertly ex   pressed in charcoal on the white plaster is a huge, looming, almost three   dimensional face of a hare, its glaring globe-eyes having been skil   fully drawn so as to appear to be reflecting the mullioned window opposite,

as well as the star skull perched atop And in casual but small neat hare there are *you run and you with the sun but* Helen admires face for a she backs out and

The sky larks' liquid jibber of song-glints has hung above Helen just to her right whilst to left the sea's shush washed some times pebbles some times sand and every then & now the curlew's bubble of call rolled

k-white ram's the log pyramid. hand-written script below the the words: *So run to catch up it is sinking.* the creature's moment. Now closes the door.

On turning to   return to a door she notices at a rear of   a building, poking from its corner, some warped planks laid on the   ground. She goes   to investigate. At a back   of a   bothy and beside these planks is an aluminium step   ladder, and beneath   the rungs of this ladder there is a short coil of blue polyprop rope. Helen retrieves this   rope and uncoils it.

Helen stands for a moment, behind the bothy, to gaze at the mountains. Again, for the umpteenth time today, the cur   lew's call wobbles somewhere o   ver the moor. As this sound   condenses almost solid on air and then dissolves to a   mist of noise and   then to silence Helen watches cloud-fibres in the sky   waver, she watches as pale light wri   thes gently across the rocky cor rugations and blue-tinged triangles of the Skyline's peaks arranged silently like, just   for this moment, the fossilised parts of some unim aginable crea   ture.

He   is wearing a filthy navy blue fleece jacket; his s t a i n e d y e l l o w

trousers are ripped at one knee; the   brown leather of his mountain boots is cracked; and the loose sole of his left boot has been cleverly strapped back in   place with wire   at the toe, the wire pas   sed through the boot's bottom two metal lace-loops and s   inched   between slots of the sole's grip.

Helen, fully aware that she is do   ing so, imagines each lay er of the distance ahead of her to throb slightly, to tick in   de- pen   dently and yet in harm   ony as if part of some sen   si- tive clock-like in   stru   ment she has made. And yet at   the same time she knows the ground & sky ahead of her, and the ocean at her side, are of course act   ually nothing she or any person could   make. With   her head cocked, slightly to her right, she stands still for a moment as if brief   ly waiting, and

as if to
perhaps
h e r
e a c h
v
S   e
yet tog

Another half-hour or so (with boots back on) of crunking along s hingle and then an other quarter of an hour (with boots back off again) of shifting footfalls across grey-yellow sand brings the bothy close to her. Helen is   struck by how throughout the last half -hour of walking along the beach she has seen no drift wood at all. Some one must've been busy collecting

s e n s e ,
through
bare feet
l a y e r ' s
ibration.
p a r a t e
ether.

At   the   c u r l e w-
c a l l ' s   fin   ish
H e l e n   glan   ces
down at the coiled rope on the ground, that she has returned to under the rungs of the stepladder ... she crouches down close, and now she can see that at one end of the rope where it pokes free from the c   oil there are a coun   table number of short bristly red hairs en   tang   led with the polyp   ro pylene's blue fibres.

There is a rusty wheelbarrow, its tyre cracked and salty, propped up just to the right of the western most window. The barrow's shadow elongates partly along the white wall and part along the cropped grass. There are very faint twines of pale blue smoke wriggling out from the top of the furthest chimney. The breeze has now subsided con side rably, and also backed by some deg rees, and so these st rings rise for the first two feet straight and then very gently curve and waver away north-eastwards.

Pink th rift nods by bou lders and the sky larks go on
and on with their un ravelling of sound, as gently yet re
lent less, elderly and fluid, Helen walks along
the coast's curve to wards the small ness of the shelter
nest led between the still stone mountains that have
waited for nothing for so long and the vast sea that for
longer still has moved for no known reasons at all
against the land's s lowly ever-chang ing edges. Helen's
body moves. Here. Along. Such an edge.

Helen chooses this windowed-door first,
sang sing that the room behind it will be
the Scotsman's re sidence. The glass rat
tles as she pushes open the door, its base
scrap ing slightly the floorboards.
Immediately Helen feels her skin prickle as
a greasy heat swells out from the room.
The heat is tinged with wood-smoke, sw
eat and cooked food. It is May, and
perhaps could be de scribed as a cool day,
but it is not the we ather for keeping a fire
in the hearth, at least during the day.

His scent of sweat & wood-s
moke mixed is str ong. With
out a word he barges past Helen
then stops. His eyes fix on her
driftwood on the ground. Now
he strides to the barrow leant
against the wall. He kicks it vi
ciously, it c langs and c latters
as it f alls scr aping the bothy
wall. Now in one jag
gedbutflowingburstofmovementhe
grabs the ror ted rubber of one
of the hand les and turns over
the cap sized barrow and then st
rides with it away down the beach
west of the both y.

probably going to be to o much.
away, that the a dult deer is
deep the little f awns
make to dra g the
the ef fort she has just had to
bothy. She knows, judging by
rags the dead body away from the
fawn's hooves, and again she p
the rope so it clasps the dead
fawn. Again she clove-hitches
walks over to the second
stretch for her right leg. Now Helen
thigh. She repeats the same
muscle down the front of her
buttock; she enjoys the stretch of
her so her heel touches her
now grasps her left ankle behind
She stands up straight again and

The bothy, now less than a hund red metres away, is placed close to the s and on a platform of sheep-cr opped grass. The grey slate roof has a brick chimney at each gable end. The south- facing white walls have two large b ay windows protruding from them. with thi ck white crossed mullions. And between these windows there is an amp le porch with a pitched s late roof. and a rob ust black door. It is actu ally quite a large bun galow cottage. Its larg eness seems to have sp routed slowly out of the gro und as she appro ached it.

She knows, after walking n ear ly eight een miles tod ay, that she will not be able to dr ag the car case any fur ther. Her legs are done. She u nties the blue p oly p rop ro pe from the hind's hin d hoo f, coils it and ret urns it to the back w all of the bo thy.

Each mile or so Helen had crouched to balance a column of pebbles, to make a teetering of stones that the most subtle of breezes could easily topple. And as this day's fresh breeze trailed her hair and flowed over her fingers she'd known her way marks were unlikely to stand. And in deed, a few times after only just a few steps Helen heard the clatter as her small freshly made precarious towers had collapsed back again amongst strewn pebbles to rejo in chaos.

Ah, time to go inside, she thin ks. Us ually on vi siting a b othy the first thin g done is to go indo ors, to ch eck out one's temp or ary ho me. But the ab rupt emergence of the young fiery Sco t sman has kept her out doors.

The dead hind bud ges only sligh tly. Now she sn atches at the rope with her full-weight and just man ages to get the mass of f lesh, bones & fur to s lide, and she keeps the moment um so the hin d slowly s kids over the prickly grass, making a soft slow velcro-z irp as its salt-clo gged fur rubs. It is easier dragging than in the sa nd, but the hind's mat ure weight stops Helen's tugging after only t went y metres. Her legs are tre mbling prof usely.

Just to the left of the door
ned food, some thirt y or
skirting board. And stacked
bay window, with their
round ends facing into the
stubby bark   less salt-
big to f it the firepl ace.
three logs for the base, then
then one on the two. Crow
of this pyram   id form is a
of its h   orns per   fectly

Now she stops, and takes a
ignoring the stink of rot. A
tugging. After an   other
or so finally she stops.
ghtly.

Helen watches his taut
the bar   row's wheel
stands staring after the
ated f   igure re   cedes
his Scottish voice ej   ects:
f   rown gent   ly wrin
turns and l   ooks down at
wo   od.

Helen cat   ches a wh iff of
as she closes in on the shel
en by an oily sweetness that
rils to t   wist and cur dle
overly strong, but Helen
is the s   mell of r   otting
just star   ting to dec   ay.
andy steps to reach the firm
red d   eer doe lying dead;
bothy's eas   tern wall, her
just below the br   east, in
pecked hole bord   ered by
ib and frin   ged by a fri

way a n   eat row of can
so tins run   ning along the
like a pyr   amid in   the
s   awn & o   pen-grained
ro   om, there   are six large
bleached logs, each far too
The stack   er has placed
two on these three, and
ning the sing   le top log
large r   am's skull, the coils
in   tact.

few slow deep gasps of air,
gain she sets to and begins
hundred & fifty met   res
Her legs are trembling sli

frame ji   g as he plo   ughs
through the sand. She
young man as his agit
down the beach. Suddenly
Fuh fux s   akes. A f   aint
kles Helen's brow, then she
her col   lection of d   rift

shar p woo   dsmoke, but
ter this scent is over   tak
s   licks through her nost
in her sto   mach. It   is not
knows the sm   ell well – it
flesh, or in this case fle   sh
And as she takes her last s
cropped grass she sees a
her spine to   uching the
eyes taken by ra   vens, and
her roun   ded belly a black
the pink-yellow edge of a r
ll of ri   pped hi   de.

And now she moves on again, continues her walk. She is barefoot, her boots with her socks stuffed in them, each strapped neatly to the sides of her rucksack. Her fig ure's shadow stretch   es tow   ards moorland to her right.

She lets sli p to the ground her rucksack & faggo t of driftwood.

She now goes over to one of the dead fawns and kneels. She c love-hitches the blue rope just above the fawn's small rear hooves, binding the spin dly hindlegs together. She stands and steps backwards till the rope comes taut, and she leans away, and begins to pow er with her legs so the fawn starts to move. The little carcase leaves a ruckled t rail in the sand as it slides. Helen wraps the rope round her waist and continues st om ping backwards, head ing east from the bot hy, tugging without pause for nearly two hun dred metres.

And now she reaches for the d o o r ' s latch ... but as she does so suddenly the door opens. In front of her in the doorway a man of about thirty stands, his light blue eyes wide & qu artz-hard, gl aring at her. His bushy beard is ginger, as is the foam of short tight curls across his scalp, as are his eyebrows crinkled under his frown. He is not as t all as Helen.

Nevertheless Helen m other and ties the her hind legs. She will week or so, as sp towards summer, the deer will make the place to try and eat soo ner it is removed will be. She stands and against the hind's in wraps the rope round ans back.

Helen enters the bothy. Beyondtheporch there is a bare room, the stonewallswhitewashed. There are a few plasticbucketsnestedtogetherandinonecorneranorang e bow-saw. There is a plank door to the right, andtotheleftapaneldoor,thetwotoprectangularpanels ofwhicharedap pled mist y glass.

kneels beside the rope to one of have a go. In a ring prog resses stink of the rotting bothy a horrible and s leep in. The the easier the job tightens the rope ert weight. She her waist and le

Helen Thorn's pack has grown heavier and become bigger. She has be en collecting driftwood for fuel, and with a length of thick elastic shock-cord she has now strapped a fag got of smooth pale bone-like sticks to her back. And Helen's face is growing a gentle sly smile – she is i mag ining how she must look now, as she plods nimbly along the shore carrying her creaking ac cidental sc ulp ture of washed tree-parts. Helen g ladly carries her faggot of sea-smoo thed fuel towards the n earing bothy.

Helen Thorn is an elderly woman, she was born before The War. Her strong legs & arms have felt the passing of many mountain days, as well as hours in cities & villages, and as well as days and nights in offices and on wards. The westerly is fresh off the sea and so her l ong silv er hair trails towards inland as she walks north towards Caul Inna-Neesh bothy. Helen is tall & straight-backed, so easily she bears the large rucksack she carries. Her stride is long and sprung. And gently her sil very hair wa vers rev ealing the pa ssing air.

The f ire place glows. And much of the room is cr ammed full of driftwood, and all gra ded neatly into stacks of sticks of varying thickness. In front of the firep lace there is a long tatter ed brown f ake-leather so fa, and on this a well-used yellow & blue down sleeping b ag. On the floorboards in fr ont of the sofa there are some light weight camping p ans & a house hold frying pan, fat sh ining in it.

She unties the rope from the hooves, and walks slowly down the beach back towards the second fawn. She pauses, stands still, and now slowly reaches down to touch her toes. She stretches the backs of her legs.

Th is lat est p art of her lif e o ver t he last f our h ours, has n ot bee n spen t but ra ther fel t. East of her t all f igure the pla ce that is no w a mo or land of he ather gr asses ree ds & bo g cot ton has b een tra nsf or ming through mill ions of y ears to ap pear now w ith its ni ne skyl arks & on e curl ew

She unstraps the bleached sticks from her rucksack, then props the sack against the porch wall. She bundles the sticks in her arms and carries them to a c   ircle of smo   ke-bl   ackened stones on sand thirty or so metres to the west of the bothy, and downwind of the dead deer. She g   lances d   own the beach after the young man, his figure is s   mall and al   most lost against the small c   rags on the far b   ank of the bur   n at the end of the beach.

She passes the dead hind to approach the porch. No no   ise sig nals her, nor   any sudden movement, but suddenly her head sw ivels tow   ards the beach to see spr   awled in the sand two dead fawns. Their tousled p   elts are clog   ged with sand. There is sand   in the sock   ets that held their eyes. The scent of s   alt off the sea & swee   t rot mix. Helen stands still, gently s   hakes her head sid   e to si   de, now carr   ies on to the por   ch door as the calls of four oy   stercatchers play the air as if for this moment the sky was a glass vibration

He   len T   horn can now make   out the little rectangle   of the bothy a   long the curving coastline. Its w   hite walls s   how clear above a g   rey-yell   ow st   rip of beach. The b   each is frin   ged by a crin   kled white fib   re of surf. Beh   ind the bothy a b   and of gree   n & br   own mo   orland, and b   eyond that, bl   uey-grey and like buck   led shee   t-steel cut-o   uts, the Black Skyl   ine stand against a ga   uze of cloud. Sunl   ight disp   ersed th   rough the gau   ze seeps so   ftly acr   oss the sgurrs' wri   nkled ga   bbro.

Smiles Balanced on Teeth

Since the first day I have had to cover my face, for the sun has looked so hard at me. I let only my eyes show. And it is not because I have a burnt face. I am not Ethiopian, my face is white – I have to hide its horrifying gleam. The Simien Mountains stitch with my footsteps, weave with my breaths – the whole rough blanket of the land seems to be made of me. The white crawling maggot of me makes the land; yet I trail through the blanket a thread of silk like a song passed by touching tongues. I thought I would be a stranger in Africa; yet it seems I am welcome, I am familiar. As I breathe hard in the high thin air, and my sweat wriggles down my face beneath my veil, I suddenly know why I am so welcome. As I struggle with the dust, struggle on the ground's surface, I realise what I am to Africa, to Ethiopia. African ground is always restless with hunger, and like any other creature I am welcome as food. I am not a stranger to this land for I am protein & fat & mineral, no different to any other protein or fat; I can be used – my death would be a small event, just another moment of refuelling something African. What a strange terror & peacefulness this is. My white friends, who still expose their faces, are a little concerned about my constantly veiling mine; but they think it is because I am burned by the sun, and as the sun is strong it's easy for me to let them think that. I cannot show my face to them, nor can I show it to the beautiful dark faces of the people of this land. The human people of this land, Abyssinians, with their wide & white-toothed smiles. How they so easily laugh, so easily joke with our wealth. Often the children make attempts to beg: 'You, you, you!', they shout, 'Pen, pen, money.' Yet it is so easy to make them smile & forget their mischief, their healthy faces are so quick to play. And yet African ground is hungry; here in these mountains there is food, but ... but Ethiopians balance their smiles on their teeth. My friends are happy to just trek through these mountains – yet now for me happiness is a trickle of silver fluid through deep red dust. My white face is naked with something about me I cannot stand. It seems I left one me in England, and then met this other one here in the highlands of Ethiopia. I have met such a strange me who is now a familiar to the ground. Yet it is only my meat & energy that is familiar to Africa; the clothes & equipment I carry are a virulent disease, a horror of infection. The high-tech fabrics with their labels bring a spore that a developing nation sucks up and multiplies. The people's weave becomes unpicked, as they forget the ground's yarns. We have all stopped walking and we are crouching, my hands touch the grass & the soil's dusty African fabrics. There is a large troop of Gelada Baboons just ahead. They don't seem to be that bothered by us though. Many of them are sitting down, some of them lift their heads up to glance at us, but they are busy at work, picking through the ground. Sometimes they crouch down to loosen roots with their teeth, but mostly they tug-&-tease the roots out with their long fingers. Their hand movements are as delicate as sewing; it is as if to feed themselves they are picking apart and skilfully altering the land's tapestry. It is like watching a nation of small furry people slowly moving over the land. They are not human, but they are people – a people perpetually & skilfully feeding themselves. Nearby, only a few metres away, there is a large male. He is facing me. The fine filaments of his fur & mane are illuminated by the sun behind him. He looks like a golden idol, but he is animated, he is not a statue. His face is a black mask; when he opens his mouth the whiteness of his teeth seems to make a bright sound. He looks at me every now & again, he is checking on me. Briefly I fold back my veil. He raises his eyebrows and his small eyes see my eyes – he sees me see him. We both know that each of us knows our eyes have been seen by the other; only people know each other like this. On his chest there is a vivid red hour-glass of bare skin, it is as if his heart is bleeding. The red skin sings its colour to the troop's females; it is an old song about new lives. But there are not many of these Gelada Baboons left, they are only found here in Abyssinia, among the Simien Mountains. It will not be long before this tiny nation of furry people is gone. These baboons with their wild voices that produce such varied & complex patterns of sounds will never get the chance to feel the pleasing weight of whole words in their mouths. I now watch a tiny dark-furred baby baboon asleep yet clinging to his or her mother's back. The babe's thin tail wraps like a vine around the thickness of the mother's. I wish I could sleep like this on Africa's ground, as tight as a vine, like this dark baby. Sleeping at altitude can be troublesome, it is common for one not to sleep well whilst acclimatising. Last night we slept at around 3700 m. But I didn't sleep. Breaths were like days; each breath a day to be planned, a clean bright airy day to be sucked into the lungs. At night to plan airy days for the lungs is hard mental work. Surely it is only God who plans days. Usually I breathe without thought; last night I breathed thoughts, burned thoughts in my blood so that I could think how to breathe-&-burn more thoughts. I dreamed, with my half open, half closed head. I dreamed without sleep. My penis tethered me to the tent floor, it was like a long leather leash; and I was a floating goat grazing on the thorns of thoughts. I saw my own face staring back at me, a grey faint metal face. And then I saw a mass of broken tents, and sleeping bags – lots of high-tech camping gear spread out on a moonlit plain. There was a tall Ethiopian wandering amongst this modern gear. He had a knarled stick and was probing with it amongst all the Gertex & Pore-Tex. His shoulders were very square, and his head seemed small & naked balanced there on his angular frame. The skin across his face was tight, his high cheek bones gleamed. His hair was a thin dark foam of curls across his skull. His eyes were direct like chips of lit quartz, yet not unkind. This man had a long robe of rags, the hem of which I felt brush across my face. He was rummaging through our bones; he was sorting through the bits of us left outside amongst useless gear abandoned on a high Afro-alpine steppe. I also remember clambering out of the tent for a pee. As I stood peeing, the freezing air rubbing round my naked legs & waist, my pee steaming, the whole sky opened its dark mouth wider than I'd ever seen before in my life. The white teeth of the stars were painfully sharp with their brightness. For the first time I saw the kite of the Southern Cross, and at the same time, on the opposite inner cheek of the vast dark mouth above me, on the sky's northern jaw I could also see the bright ivory points of The Plough. In the sky's mouth the dark soil of the heavens was being turned over whilst a kite resisted heaven's dark breath. I am standing on the very edge of the escarpment. The escarpment is the most striking geological feature of the Simien Mountains. Below me a solidified sea of earth & rock waves rolls away into haze; and I am standing on the crest of its biggest wave, a motionless tsunami. The cliff falls directly for 300 metres and then slopes steeply for 2000 metres more into the valleys below. I am balanced on the edge of this vast tooth, and the sky is smiling. Amongst the haze on the horizon there is a quivering orange fruit; a blaze sinking into the night, like the Ark of the Covenant being carried away. Suddenly a Lammergeyer swoops past me. He is close enough for me to hear the air pass prayers through his golden breast feathers. I can see the polished coffee bean of his eye, and the dark taste of his gaze. His outstretched wings are nailed to the swift air. He grips in his talons a thigh-bone. He circles up-&-away from me, my neck hurts now as I crane upwards. He lets the thigh-bone go, a white letter I (or figure 1) plummets then explodes bone-sparks on rocks. The Lammergeyer is now picking through the fragments for marrowbone. I can feel his beak in my thigh; it is like I'm being ripped into. But he is over there, not here with me – he is eating some other creature's remnants. Perhaps I am a prophet! Blasphemy, like something a mosquito injected into me, seems to be developing in my system. This high up in the mountains, on the top of Africa, it is easy to feel like a prophet. I have come to deliver my message to the nation of Giant Lobelia. They stand around me, their long light-green tongue-like leaves rattling in the breeze. It's as if their green heads were each made of many large stars of David bound together to make a globe. I address old Abyssinian Jews, or green ghosts of Jews – Falashas frozen in lignin & xylem. The Giant Lobelia are crowding around me. I speak with them, I deliver my prophecy. My words fall on deaf green ears. But I speak on: "Beware the muscular goat! Beware the Walia Ibex. Yea, behold this image: The orange coated beast; the black & white striped stockings; the swept-back horns proud as an ancient ship's bows. I say unto thee: Surely it is within this goat-ship, within this ark of bones & muscles that the transparent stones of God reside. Behold: The Ibex with a tongue of green; a tongue of Lobelia leaf that slowly recedes into its mouth as it eats. Lo, Africa digests all peoples. O, Giant Lobelia be weak – that is your true strength! Be soft in the breeze, for strength is hardness – and hardness is a partner of death." I am suddenly aware of just how blasphemous a mosquito it must have been that drilled me. I move closer to the escarpment's edge, so that the toe of one of my boots hangs above open air. To my left the cliff edge juts out as a promontory. Suddenly on the promontory there is a movement: a creature appears. On a small ledge thrust out into the air, above the brown valleys, balanced on an edge – a magnificent male Walia Ibex has taken a stance. His stiff black beard below his chin is like a paint brush pointing downwards, and his stiff tail is like a black paint brush pointing upwards. He is huge, nearly as tall as I am. His ribbed horns have an agile weight – they cut open the air as he turns his head to gaze at me. Now he plummets, he drops a full 3 metres to another tiny ledge. He is cantering along a ramp that I would take many minutes to traverse. I hear his hooves clatter like leather bells. He rushes as if the sight of him is a secret. Suddenly he is being followed by a whole herd. It is as if an orangey brown river of Ibex were falling down the cliff, they gush from the edge of the promontory. Many of them are whistling warnings at each other because of my presence. I am filled with an urge to shout "Moses!" at the ship-like male Ibex suddenly far below me leading the way. Some of these muscular goats glance back up at me. The herd gracefully falls away into the depths below the great wave of the escarpment. Their size diminishes until they are a faint orange school of fishes darting away into the shadows of the land's ocean. It is time for us to turn away from the high ground. I have decided that we must go a more unusual way back, we must not return the same way. It is time to veer away from the neat red dots of the Swiss map, away from the trekkers' route, from the make-believe & fake. It is time to no longer be blasphemous. It is time to eat my own words. We should stalk, we should return cunningly. We will descend a remote valley little frequented by white faces. And I will face my fate. But it is not bravery like Gawain's that urges me to face fate; it is actually my very facelessness, my eaten nakedness that fascinates Africa's inevitable gravity. Abyssinia will take my face and burn it in her digestive tract.

I have woken this morning to find I have written a poem. I cannot recall writing it, and it doesn't seem to be in my handwriting. Someone is speaking to me in Amharic; it is a woman's voice. The words, which I cannot understand, are sweet like honey, but also slightly rough like honey with fragments of hard bee & hive crushed in amongst its softness. The Amharic has an Arabian smell to it, it is like smoke curling out of her mouth. And yet Africa is the fire that drives the Amharic smoke from the dark woman's beautiful receptive mouth. The cup of her mouth overflows with an oil of vowels & smoke of consonants. Two rods of cold carved rock could be placed in her grail – but here such stone has no script, it is blank. Void of commandment. She is singing so sweetly in Amharic. The cool Afro-alpine air is vibrating with her voice. I will read my poem as she sings. I am suddenly filled with a desire for her, a need like Solomon's for Sheba. I am trying so hard to write a Song of Songs for her, but I only have this poem:

To Plant to Pitch

mountains ground dreams rhythms

seeds glow

$$\underline{\bar{b}}$$

hungry meat event
ground tongue syllables

bone sun

$$\underline{\bar{e}}$$

Abyssinia Africa

seeds see smiles' teeth

$$\underline{\bar{r}}$$

soup tear
tired miles

ground smiles soup

food burst me

weak

eat blood weep dreams!

$$\underline{\bar{o}}$$

water vanishing

dust whiten!

ᚼ

land engravings skin me

ground takes away free dreams

swirl plughole!

ʒ̄

hollow lit west

silhouette skeleton

I have a sudden feeling of elation, and freedom. We are now descending into the Belegez Valley. We are leaving behind Chennek and the escarpment. I have no doubts about the beauty & magnificence of this high ground that we are now leaving; but it is somehow tainted by the Swiss map and the brash European trekkers that follow the map's red dots. I suddenly feel as if I have stepped into a real Africa. There is no doubt that hungry Africa was always there as we trekked the usual way, but it was overlaid by a copy of Africa. I have a faint feeling of trespass about my boots. Yet I also feel that we have the permission of our scout, Isaac. Isaac, who although now not sure of the way, seems to use his Kalashnikov assault riffle as some kind of broomstick or compass – when he holds it it doesn't seem like a modern weapon of war. And although we white ones read the Swiss map and its contours he does not fully understand, Isaac nevertheless stands still in the land as it passes peacefully beneath his feet. One of my white friends, whose name I cannot remember, and whose face seems to be fading – he is trying to see behind my veil. I know we have been friends in England for many years, but now I only know this like a scientist knows about atoms. I lash out at him. There is no way that I can allow anyone to see behind my veil. I now walk some way behind the rest of the party, and I think they feel glad for that. I am sorry for them, but this me that I have met does not behave like me – I cannot help me. The valley walls are steep, but are dotted with round mud huts and spread with terraced fields. There are many strawstacks, often perched in knarled olive trees. The straw is bright & golden; the stacks are like heaps dug from Solomon's mines. We left the Giant Lobelia line sometime ago; I look back at a nation of still green stars on stalks, I can just make out their ranks high up at the head of the valley. We are descending so quickly. We pass a young man ploughing; he is shouting at his cattle urging them through centuries of work in one afternoon whilst the single shiny plough share writes its requests in the ground. How quickly we are going down – are we trying to keep up with the river? For a moment I'm sure I see another see-through me rushing ahead trying to pull me on, in fact more than one other me, many of them. I feel like stretched liquid afraid of being dried out under the sun. We must slow down. The valley has now begun to widen and level out, the floor is flat & luxuriantly green next to the river. Mercifully we rest. I am sitting with my back against the cream-coloured trunk of a huge sycamore fig tree. Her branches snake away above me. The whole tree is surrounded by a circular dry-stone wall. I feel as if I'm in the cool shade of a church, light slanting like streamers of bronze foil through the church's wide-reaching snaky eaves. I am sitting under a vast skirt. So peaceful. But suddenly the church is invaded – we are besieged by a group of riotous & gleeful children. They are dressed in brightly coloured rags, with many patches. The big stitches on their patches, done in colours that clash, seem like instructions – seem like paths marked on maps. The children are shouting English "Hello!"s. I notice one tiny child has a can ring-pull on her necklace, whilst another's necklace holds the top half of a small toothpaste tube. Some of the children want to see behind my veil, I am trying to fend off two particularly inquisitive individuals. Suddenly there is a coughing yelp from one of the children. She must've caught a glimpse of my face. Now the rest of what was a happy crowd are running away, out from beneath the sycamore fig, there are screams & tears. My white, and now fading ghost-like friends, and also the scout are looking at me oddly. They are suspicious. I turn to run, I run out from under the sycamore fig's many arms, I run out into the white & hot sunlight, I run down the valley. I am running running. My boots have split; I look down to see the expensive Italian leather fall away from my feet, or what were my feet. My feet are white transparent stones, they are made up of horribly white rods of stone. I hold up my hands to the sun. I can see through them. I am suddenly tumbling down a steep bank. And now I am waist deep, sitting in the Belegez river. The water is washing away my clothes. There is a young Abyssinian woman bathing just metres away from me. I can see her bare back gleaming chestnut-brown in the sun. As she turns towards me I am overwhelmed by the swing of her breasts, and the full curve of her belly. She is pregnant. She does not seem bothered by me. Her eyes are sparkling, sparkling as if millions of electric fish swam in her vision. She smiles at me, but I can see that there is pity in her smile. Then I notice my reflection. I cannot pull my face away from the reflection of my face in the river. My veil is dissolving like smoke, my face is stuck to the flowing reflection, my face is forever flowing. And I have no eyes. And the flowing reflection suggests that my face is somewhere else in the form of a hard horribly bright white translucent stone – a gleaming tooth on which nothing is written.

The Ewe Stone

nothing-&-stone mingle wind – Holly North

The middle-aged man stared at the rock just in front of his face. The toe-tips of his mountain boots were snug on a thin lip of stone. As he balanced, and gazed at what he was balancing on, the stone's rugosities stayed utterly still, as they had done for hundreds of millions of years.

Yet the man found himself making these solid ripples change shape; he saw a continent's outline, and a goat's head, and then the hungry grimace of some strange un-known beast ... which then caused him to recall the little church towards the valley's mouth, five miles away and two thousand feet or so below. Beside the church yard's single yew tree there was a roughly hewn Celtic cross, and below the cross a small face-shape with a hole in it, no doubt meant to be a mouth. He did not lose contact with the hard ancient substance he was climbing on, but so very briefly one of his carefully placed feet slid ever-so slightly along the stone lip. He rebuked himself for letting his mind go astray. He was not used to losing his concentration. He needed to stay focused. The climbing was not desperately hard, but the rock was becoming greasy.

It was twelve years ago that he was last here. He had thought the climb would be a pleasant remembering. But a niggling doubt had crept down the back of his neck. He was also a man not used to doubt.

The ragged ridge of the fell across the valley had grown a grey fur of cloud. He watched it swell to a wavering gauze of moist air that started to creep down the craggy slopes opposite. He was alone, and un-roped. Perhaps he should've waited a day or two more, waited for more settled weather.

Holly would've waited. She was a bold climber, and nothing much worried her, but she was also patient, and would always think carefully ahead. Whereas he would rely on his few gifts: physical precision & agility on all kinds of ground be it clean rough stone or algae-stained slabs or friable walls or decrepit ice. And he had uncommon stamina, and an appetite for, as he often called it: Simply ballsing it out.

A few straightforward moves brought him to a small ledge. The toe of his right boot nestled under a few fronds of heather. The heather held a constellation of bright droplets that jiggled as he moved his foot. Again, he rebuked himself. The little jewels were a distraction, and not what he was used to paying his attention to. He turned to look down the valley. The white thread of the beck wriggled. And the grey gauze on the fellside opposite had fattened further into a tumbling mass of hairy mist – it quickly engulfed each outcrop it fell past. In all his years of being amongst mountains he had never seen hill-fog move with such sullen weight.

He felt stupid and annoyed with himself. It was just weather, and *weather was the medium through which the mountaineer moved* ... that was all it was. He was imagining things.

He looked straight down at the little ragged-edged tarn at the base of the crag. It shimmered gently as slanting sunlight skidded its surface. The path beside the tarn, that led back down towards the beck – the neat inevitability of its threading its way around knolls & craglets was as comforting as a familiar story. He heard a faint *cuck-ooo cuck-ooo* rise up from somewhere far down the valley. Briefly he thought he caught on the slight breeze a whiff of fresh-mown grass. They were cutting for silage in the bigger fields, just before the bridge over the beck where the lane crossed and went on up to the church.

He looked up the crag. He clearly remembered the tricky section just ahead, which led to the arête overlooking the dark cleft of the North Gully. The pitch followed a shallow groove full of vertical curving ripples like water on a wind-blown tarn. The ripples looked deceptively positive, but when you reached them they turned out to be smooth as adders.

That's the way she put it. And he remembered her wry smile, and the direct sweet lance of her gaze as she said it. He hadn't thought of that moment in years, but here it was. He smiled to himself. His anger and the strange niggling that had crept down his spine since setting foot and fingers on this crag, it subsided a little. She was always so good at calming him down.

He had climbed the 'groove of adders' a number of times, and once he'd even done it whilst pound-coin-sized snowflakes ticked on his hood and blurred the rock. Today the ripples were cool and greasy, nothing he was not used to. A dry *crock-crock* suddenly cracked gently in his ear, and through his eye-corner he caught the black flickering flag of a raven slide down the sky past him. The bird's agility and brilliance inspired him. He set to.

The man leant away from one of the sharper ripples, the finger-skin of both hands pressed hard, pulling against the rock. He carefully plugged the front rim of his left boot into one of the hip-like curves of the thickest ripple. His right foot had nothing much to stand on. This was the move, at least of this pitch. In front of his nose now, a stringy black beetle crawled across one ripple and then up and down another. It scurried so swiftly that he thought he saw a tiny dark horse galloping over silver hills. For an instant the beetle's back had glinted. He felt the left boot begin to fade. The grip – the contact – that usually felt like a tight wire running from his toe up his leg and into his stomach, where he would feel it and pull it neatly with his gut muscles ... suddenly the tension dissolved. The grip's crispness melted. The beetle had disappeared. He let out a growl and cursed himself. His foot was slipping. And he was frightened. He could feel his planet's mass pulling at him. He had not felt fear like this ever before.

He was falling ... and then he was somehow on the rock again and his limbs making blurred movements and his fingertips feeling out a quick repetition of tapping and scrapes his breathing thick liquidy bag-fulls of gasps eyes wide open but what he saw was just stone-coloured shapes wavering all that was happening and all he did was governed by touch.

He had reached the easy angled arête overlooking the North Gully. He stood trembling on big holds. He could hardly recall the last few moments, he simply could not account for how he was now still alive. His years of experience and consolidated skill must've suddenly kicked in, he must've switched to some kind of 'automatic'. He was partly amazed at what his body had just done, yet he had never climbed so badly. He yelled, You fuckwit! *Wit!* echoed back at him, out from the deep gully to his immediate right.

He turned to look down the valley; he could see nothing of it, he was now surrounded by a moist grey swirling slightly-luminescent floss. The heather on the ridge opposite, across the gully, was bathed in a shiny grey fluid, and was as still as if it had been carefully carved out of metal into astounding intricacy. Yes, the heather and the grasses were absolutely still, he was sure of it; yet he could feel a strong breeze rushing up past his ears, he could hear the straps on his rucksack gently clattering. He felt a lone raindrop splat on his scalp. Then there was another. Then. Another. He could feel cold water wriggling amongst his hairs. Now one drop rolled what he imagined as a silvery pulsating trail down his nape under his fleece and into the warm middle of his back. And then he found himself seeing – or was it somehow feeling? – raindrops falling upwards blown off his skull in the updraft. He shook his head and scrunched his eyes. And he swore again and his voice again bounced back at him out of the gully. He needed to pull himself together. What the hell was wrong with him?

Think of Holly. He brought her face into focus her green eyes kind yet dangerously sharp the glint in each of those eyes clear as a star-point shot across space like a lighthouse pulse on a horizon a sign of safety and yet also of danger. He suddenly realised that's what it was – that exquisite mixture of uncertainty ... and trust. He smiled to himself again. He listened to her voice. She was banging on again about poetry ... but he was listening now. She was talking about Coleridge, describing excitedly yet precisely as if she had been there with the poet, how he lay down and writhed on Scafell's rocky ground as thunder raged round him and lightning ... it never actually struck his body, but it electrocuted something deep down in the dark of him, made a crisp shadow of something never seen before suddenly loom on the inside of his dazzling skull. She talked about climbers today, and how easy it is when you know so many have done these things before you, or at least things similar if not quite as hard. But Coleridge, no one had ever done anything like he did. That descent of Broad Stand ... he could hear her clearly and he listened to her properly for the first time as she described that descent hold by hold she detailed the feel of each shape made by the ancient rock as that foolish yet somehow wise poet touched the mountain's stone.

And then he remembered where he was now standing: on slick rock in pouring rain on an arête some three hundred feet above the little tarn mouthing its silent grey gasp lost in the mist below. And he was nothing like focused, his brain was carrying on in all directions. A wave of anger rolled through him and then broke ferociously. He screamed into the gully. No words. Just thick tangled wire strands of sound fell out of his mouth and then jabbed back at him bounced off the gully's walls.

He needed to get moving, and needed to move well. He had sixty or so feet ahead of him before the broad ledge, and after that just scrambling up the ridge. But, the last twelve-foot of climbing before the sanctuary of the ledge was harder than 'the adders' ... and in this rain and in big boots ... He wished he'd brought rockshoes, but then rockshoes would be useless now. His mind roamed around for ideas. He had no oversized woollen socks with him that he could pull over the mountain boots, the fibres of which would help him grip the soaked slippery stone.

He tried to focus, and calm his anger ... but again an ocean roller of rage crashed over him. He was stupid, for blundering into this trap, this rock-trap, no, this middle-aged, no, senile mind-trap. Again he threw his insult into the gully – Fuckwit! – and waited a fraction of a second before again half the word rebounded on him. *Wit!*

He now wanted nothing more than to get away as quickly as possibel. He tensed himself. Pulled the buzzing wires of his heart tight and connected the wires of his muscles to the beating centre of him. He looked straight up the crag, at the rock to come. But as he craned his neck upwards something seemed to flare in the corner of his right eye. His senses were acute, his feelings wriggled to points. He was about to move upwards. But. He stopped.

Over to his right, across the gully ... earlier on he thought he'd seen a perched boulder on the ridge, a boulder he'd never noticed before, but thought nothing of it ... he could see now that it wasn't a boulder at all – it was a dark grey sheep, probably a ewe, but oddly he wasn't sure. Of course it was a ewe, a tup wouldn't be up here high on the fell. Whatever, it was standing stock still. On thick hoar-frosted legs. And it was staring at him. He found himself staring back at it. The black grooves in its eyeballs pulsated a thick unintelligible but somehow knowing message. He pulled his eyes away from its gaze, and carefully observed the beast. Yes, the horns were polled, so a yowe it was, but a large one. In fact she was as big as any tup, Herdwick or otherwise, he'd ever seen. Actually, she seemed bigger than any tup he'd seen. She was huge. And she was statue-still, yet her gaze propelled a fluid energy. Her rugged bluey grey wool held droplets of rain. She was certainly living: wisps of steam rose from her underneath to writhe delicately in the woollen canyons of her fleece. Then suddenly she shook, a rolling neck-to-rump-wave like a dog's shake, flinging droplets off of her. And then she was utterly still again. Staring.

As a boy he'd worked at least four of his summers on his uncle's remote farm, right up towards the head of Detterdale, over on the Western edge of The District. He knew exactly what Herdwicks looked like, and he knew something of their moods, and knew their postures, and most of their ways of going about the fells. Over the years, and in all seasons wandering the fells, he'd gained an affection for the beasts. Their sturdy woollen legs, and sure-footedness. Their wide, somehow kind and almost religiously resigned faces. And their simply sticking it out and going on with things, busily methodically cropping the wiry fell grasses with wind ruffling their fleeces or even snow gathering on their backs. Funny, he'd never thought these things so clearly before. Holly would've made a sarcastic but sweet comment about these thoughts. She would've approved.

But the beast now gazing at him, this creature had none of that Herdwick kindness. It was the same breed for sure, but this one, she was so big. And her stare ... her stare seemed malevolent. He was being bloody stupid again. If this was the Rockies and that was a mountain goat, well perhaps he had something to be wary of. But no, this was just a sheep. And besides, there was a broad gully between him and it.

He started laughing, his cackle resonating in the gully, and he began to recall how a goat in Corsica had indeed bucked him and knocked him off the mountain path he was on. How he had laughed as the goat came at him its dangling ears flapping the surprise comedy of it all the thud of its skull against his thigh and how Holly and Jerry had laughed too and even as he was rolling down the scree he couldn't help spewing out big gulps of clattering laughter laughter at the joyful daftness of having been flicked off a mountain by a brown nanny goat. He was a very young man then, and despite tumbling some two hundred feet down steep scree he hardly hurt himself at all. After scrabbling back up to the others he proudly showed them his only wound – red jewels dripping off the point of his elbow, glittering in the cool blue air.

This wasn't funny though. Again he realised his mind had just taken leave of his body, and had started wandering all over the shop. And again he wanted to curse and yell, but this time remembered his voice rebounding back at him from the gully. He kept silent. All the noise he'd so far made had made no difference to the beast. The stony ewe absolutely still was still there. She stared at him. Yes, he was certain, she *was* actually staring at him. And she seemed to know it.

He needed to move, and he needed to move so very very well. He could feel the ewe's eyes on him. He glared upwards at what was to come. And strangely that animal gaze from across the way – he held it somewhere in the back of his head and somehow he connected it to the wiry pulsating mass of his heart and the wires of precision tightened in him and he was there now suddenly there at the crux the horribly slippery rock and small wrong-way-pointing holds all in his power and he could see his fingers crisply in focus and feel the delicate pattern of friction under the weather's grease and he watched himself it seemed six or so feet away from and behind himself and he climbed the soaking pitch better than he'd climbed any pitch ever before.

He stood on the big ledge. It was more of a deep bay, a balcony of expansive safety. The gully was no longer in view, the bay's tall right wall obscured it. The surrounding walls offered some shelter from the weather, but every now and again a buffet of wind spiralled in and then spiralled out. And the rain was no longer falling straight down, instead the wind had set it aslant, or if not aslant it momentarily spattered as gusts swirled it. And the rain was becoming sticky with floppy grey crystals. His hands were raw with cold. When he'd started this climb it was spring, and yet it was now November. He stood still, statue-still he thought. He stood on the vast ledge astounded to be there.

Whatever the bloody ewe wanted with him, somehow he'd got the better of it, used his indignation at the absurdity of her. That was it, that was what he'd done. He wasn't even sure if there had even been a ewe. No. There hadn't, of course that was it, yes! – he'd made the whole damn thing up to get him out of his fix. He'd read of such motivating hallucinations in tales of mountaineering daring-do. He smirked. He felt silly. Sheepish indeed. He heard himself laugh his forced guffaw streaming out a fraying stringy trail as the wind picked it up and took it away.

He looked beyond the big ledge up the remaining ridge. The scrambling was blocky, spiky and festooned with holds. But the soppy crystals now being squeezed out of the woollen sky were blunting the spikes and filling the holds and smearing the rock. The wind speed was picking up. The scramble was not going to be a doddle. But it'd go. It would, of course, have to.

His legs felt as if the gathering sleet-sludge was already up to his thighs. He looked down, it was only a centimetre thick, if that. A thin layer was gathering on the tops of his boots. But his legs felt stuck, as if his own muscles were huge slugs clamped to his bones, frozen to his bones. He was knackered, more knackered than he'd ever been. More goosed than when he'd topped out on McKinley after days of vertical, brutal mixed ground, and in howling wind. How could that be?

Denali, it's called Denali not bloody McKinley! He heard her voice mix momentarily into swift wet air. She had quite a deep voice but with a bright edge. A slight sing that dissolved in amongst the throaty yet mellow notes of her turns of phrase. And she sometimes had such odd but just-so ways of saying things. He should've said as much to her. Her voice fell back in amongst the background hiss of wind and dwindled and then was gone.

He felt bewildered – a cold hollow growing in his gut. He recalled the image of the ewe. Stone-still still staring. Then a slicing

pang of fright as if an icicle had been pushed under his ribcage. The cold-razor ache fanned out up his chest and settled in his throat. He gulped cold. Leaning against the ledge's largest rhyolite block there was a figure. Stupidly he had expected the ewe to appear from the small cave at the back of the bay ... and in the instant he dismissed this ridiculous fear the large block that dominated the ledge seemed to grow a tall shape out of its flank. There was a man leaning against the stone. There actually was a man.

Keeping his eyes on the figure, he knelt. Then he bowed his head and fixed his gaze to the ground. He pressed a palm into the rock's cold undulations, then lifted the hand and thwacked it down again to test his world's solidness. His hand buzzed with the impact, but it felt real and that was good. He squeezed his eyes shut. He looked like a man in the starting blocks, or some big cat about to look up and then pounce. When he opened his eyes the bay would be empty. The side of the big block would be empty – the block would only be gathering the air's wet snow.

He opened his eyes. Wide. Immediately his body pulled into its lungs a thick soaked rope of air. His gasp's hiss outstripped that of the wind. The man had not gone. The figure was still there.

This other man, leaning against the block, suddenly stood upright. He was wearing a grey suit, a thin black tie against a white shirt. He had on brown brogues. Of course the suit was ruined, completely soaked. All down the left arm there was a dark green smear of algae. And the outside seam of the trousers' left leg had split to the knee. The wet rag flapped each time a gust curled round the bay. But the figure didn't seem much bothered by the state of his clothes. Claggy snow gathered on the man's broad shoulders and flecked his wavy black hair. He was a young man, but with a direct steady gaze that seemed to pass across an ancient distance. The dark eyes were set deep below thick eyebrows. The nose was prominent and slightly hooked, giving the young pale face a hawkish precision. The lips were thin but distinct and strong. And the young man's jaw was large and square.

Then this younger, yet somehow decades older man spoke: *In a huge, open-wide, leaping eye of a bear   A mountain gleams in the pupil.* His accent had been formed in Yorkshire. The voice was at once gritty and yet smooth like river moving. *I see the dark pool   In the snow   On that huge hill   But I cannot see   If its water's full   Of foetus or food.* There was a slight tremble as the syllables bled precisely from between the thin lips. But the tremble in the voice, although making the middle-aged man think of fear, was not at all a tremble of weakness, it was more the kind of wavering resonance made by a massive bronze bell. *That meaningless cry with its sea-voice   Churning equally its dead-&-alive.* And yet at the same time there was a distinct glimmer of gentleness in the voice, and a reassuring certainty, as if each word had been given like a pebble, pressed into the palm, unpolished by cloths, but already gleaming. Perhaps the words were polished only by the wind. *Your climbing   Your climbing   Slides my skeleton slowly through space.*

Now the young man smiled. It was not too dissimilar to one of Holly's more mysterious smiles, the one that would make him feel judged sharply and yet at the same time collude with him.

That's a good thought! the young man said to him. Yes, she colludes with you. All those words of hers lace the air. Even now she tightens your ears to feel. *Here is her gesture   Here is her fern   Hear her unfurl.* The steady yet wavering yet stony yet watery voice let loose its sounds to be caught by the sleet-speckled air to be torn away and torn up and mixed in and lost amongst uncountable atoms of elements:

Meaningless living appearance:
Night's self-pebble.

Universe sleep – sun's foetus.

The wind with nothing.
The stone's directions.

Sea to fallen conditions;
Her aeon develops.

Variant angels bow.

The old eyes in the young man's face kept locked on the other man's. Then turned away. And swiftly as a deer startled or hawk stooping the tall drenched grey-suited figure leapt away from the large block and was then on the bay's tall dark-green-greasy right wall making crisp person-shapes & gestures-of-clinging and balancing and pushing and connecting these gestures into one single fluid alphabet of motion up the impossibly hard wall. Then the figure was gone.

This was too much. He simply was not going to accept this. He smacked his forehead repeatedly, whispering: Stupid! Stupid! Stupid! He could hardly tell if the whispers came from his throat or if they were wind curling in his ears.

Quickly he got stuck into the final scramble leading up the ridge. He made no decisions. His body simply carried its small heat glimmering within him over the slippery blocks as the grey rumbling syrupy wind wrapped its sleet-tendrils round his frame and tried to pull or push him off the mountain. But the wind could not.

The sleet had now fluffed to snow. The climb was behind him. He staggered through feathery roiling flakes. The light was odd – bright then shadowy sweeping swathes as gaps in higher-up clouds opened and closed. He knew the ground ahead: a little plateau of craglets & knolls. But the wavering snow-strands and sudden twisters of speckled air put contorted veils and masks in front of familiar shapes. The slanting light was fading; it was much later than he'd planned.

And then on the close horizon, on a knoll, pixelated by the laden air, there it was again. No! No, that could be any ewe. It wasn't the same. It disappeared for an instant into the weather, than came back crisp as sudden sunlight edged it. He squinted back at it, its shape fading in and out of this granular world he had suddenly found himself in. But even at this distance, some hundred metres, and through the hiss-interference, he could see, or perhaps feel, the eyeballs' deep black stripes pinned on him. It was the same ewe.

He pushed ahead in amongst the knolly ground. He was looking for the narrow tarn. Once he found that he could be certain of his position. The reed tussocks and rough grass were bristling with clinging flakes. Whenever he hit boggy ground each squelched step seeped back black wet through the settling snow. As he moved amongst the undulations he glimpsed twice more the shape of the ewe. She was following.

This was the place: he rounded the little pyramid crag dappled with deep pockets. He stood at the entrance to a small corridor of flat ground nestled amongst the plateau's craggy hummocks. And lying spirit-level-flat and black the length of this geological lane was the narrow tarn. From where he stood the corridor ran south to north, and was well sheltered from the cold easterly. He stepped in. The place was hushed and felt almost indoors compared to the surrounding windswept land. The black water rippled gently as white falling flecks vanished through its membrane. Here and there the tarn was frilled with spiky reeds, all gathering falling crystals. And intermittently as the strange light pulsated its swathes of gleam and shade the tarn's skin would buzz swarms of glisten and then suddenly snap back silent and blacken so the falling specks again were seen clearly passing from air into abyss. Carefully he moved along the tarn's edge. Then stopped.

At the other end of the corridor, ahead of him, she was there again. He simply turned his back on her.

He stood absolutely still, statue-still he decided. And he ignored the absurdity. He listened to the sough of flakes and the glossy glugging at the tarn's edge, and beyond that the wind rubbing along rocks and snowy grass. And then he could hear a sudden acceleration of hooves. He tried to think of other things, but he found the sound of a horse cantering into gallop. And then a bear's steaming sawing roar-&-grimace loomed through his mind, his entrails hot with terror. And now a wolf's howl. And wolves' snouts jabbing at him, and rows of slick glinting teeth gripping his flesh. The rumbling hooves were gaining. He could no longer ignore it. He spun round and instantly the ewe's head with a flick hard & precise as a goat's thumped into the side of his left knee and dragged up his thigh and took his feet from under him he was wheeling round sideways an iciness suddenly clamping round him up to his waist. And then she was gone.

Fuuuck! fuuck! fuck! He dragged himself out of the tarn, and tried to stand, and tried to rub and squeeze away the water from his trousers. He didn't think anything was broken, but his right knee – suddenly the ligaments were vibrating horribly and a deep dull ache bloomed through bone.

And then the middle-aged man began laughing. There he was alone in the snowy wind soaking wet by a black tarn a sheep had just flicked him into. He bent over with his right hand on his good knee, and he laughed huge gulps. And then just as quickly as his laughing had begun, it left him, as if the wind had instantly sucked out of him the rippling rhythm of his laughter and he was left spent.

He flopped down to sit in the snowy grass, then immediately stood up again and made the effort to take off his rucksack, and then sat back down on that. He sat for minutes with his jaw cupped by his right hand and his elbow propped on his good knee, and he stared at the black water wobbling gently just a few feet in front of him. He felt the wet cold round his legs and loins cling. Then the ache in his knee was like some kind of burning light, but when he looked down at it there was no light at all, just his outstretched leg with snow settling on it. He stared into the black water hardly noticing his juddering muscles protesting the cold. He stared. And a pressure within him and from without was immense and pinned him to the moment. If he closed his eyes now he would sleep. He blinked. Then rubbed his eyes with his wet knuckles.

He had a fair way to go to get down to the valley, and then back to his car parked by the church. Even in decent weather there was a good two hours in it, at least without running. But with his knee and being soaked in this wind, and what with the increasing snow and the decreasing light ... and this feeling so utterly spent and not knowing why .... he knew he was actually in trouble. Here in the little hills not many miles from his childhood home ... how odd that after all it was these little hills that would take him.

Instantly he heard Holly rebuke him. He turned round to see behind him. Of course, no one was there. But yes, what the hell was he thinking? He could never have imagined that he of all people could've simply sat down and given up on his life. We need a plan, Batman! And he saw her smile again. But even though he wanted so much to reach into the falling crystals and the limitless air and embrace her and tumble away across some incomprehensible ancient distance ... he resisted. She smiled at him, warmly.

And so he was now back on task, and soon he'd be bang on target, he had to be, he had to get packing, and he had to get up, and had to just go. For a moment he cast around for a cunning plan, and then he remembered. Yes, Holly and he had once winter-climbed the North Gully.

They had set off in foul weather, and when they topped out it was full blizzard. They had huddled together next to the narrow tarn, which was thick-lidded with ice, snowflakes swishing over it. And he had started to wonder how the hell they were going to get back; the wind was so ferocious, and the sharp speeding crystals vicious. He'd suggested crawling back to the gully, but they had climbed ropeless, and down-climbing amongst growing spindrift didn't look good. No problemo! she said, for she had spotted on the map, weeks before, a small remote building in the next valley along, not too far away from the narrow tarn. On the map, next to the building's square black outline the cartographer had drawn a single tiny pale green pine. She'd then visited this little stone building and found it hunkered amongst five Scots pines. And its roof was good and it was full of hay. She had led the way to this shelter, both of them often forced to crawl through the snow under the wind's rumbling lid. When they opened the little barn's door, and then shut it tight again behind them, they stepped instantly from pitiless storm into a peaceful den filled with the sweet smell of dried grass.

He needed to forget the ewe. He had to put everything into pushing on towards the barn. He needed to find the faint path that led eastwards out of the knolls to open fellside. It was four hundred-ish metres further north from the north end of the tarn. Then after following the path for half a K or so, he'd have to leave it to find the top of the scree gully that would take him quickly down the north facing fellside into the barn's lonely valley. There were a few little cairns along the path, and there was a distinct elbow as the path crossed a crease in the hillside. It was at the elbow that he should leave for the scree gully. In his mind the images of the ground ahead were distinct, as were the images of the map of the area that he'd studied often, but long ago ... and he would've said that once he knew the ground fairly well, but still he couldn't account for such detailed clarity of recollection.

By now the sun had set, and the greyness of the air began to tinge with thickening purple. The tarn was behind him, he limped northwards following his compass. His eyes strained at the grey-white ground with each step. He was waiting for the path; he had to be ready to pick out the thread of it amongst the thickening flakes scurrying through the grasses.

And then he was there – the small cone of a cairn suddenly resolved in front of him. He was blessing whatever luck had found him and put him by the cairn when the ewe that he'd tried so hard to forget was suddenly again standing. In front of him. Still. As when he'd first seen her on the ridge across the North Gully. Earlier in the day. A day. That already as he was. Finishing it seemed. From long. Long ago. She was just twenty feet away from him. Still. Staring.

He really did think he'd imagined her. Despite his buckling knee and the pain, and the memory of the bone of the ewe's head connecting with the bones of his leg, he really did think he'd imagined her. Anger rose in him as if a collie had nipped the top of his calf. The ewe just stood still. Staring. Be off with you you fucker! He waggled his arms at her furiously, and wailed like a wolf. She stood. Then in a single ratchety motion he staggered-and-stooped-and-scooped-up a stone from the cairn and as he stood straight again pushing up most of his weight with his good leg he swung his arm and let loose the stone towards his target. The precision of his shot shocked him. The stone made a sharp hollow *clat* as it impacted with her snout. Instantly blood bloomed from her nostril. She bowed her head and pawed at the pain with her hoof. Black drops spotted amongst grass tips poking through snow. And some black strands dangled down the wind. Then the ewe lifted her eyes to him once more before she bleated her stony *baah* and then turned from him and bounded away her woollen rump bouncing back up towards the knolls in the direction of the narrow tarn her grey shrinking shape quickly brushed away by the streaming wall of scratchy flakes.

He stood and stared after her. Stared into the grey swish of speckled veils backed by purpling shadows. He could see nothing more of her. And he suddenly felt sorrow and was ashamed. He thought of his uncle's ewes. And guilt suddenly crawled into him. She was, of course, just a sheep.

The stippled wind's sting pressed against his face. He followed along the stringy path, and found the elbow in it. And then soon after that in darkness his headtorch jiggling its beam through flecks he speedily skidded and rode down the snow-muffled clatter of the scree descending an ancient escalator away from the higher ground holding the black narrow level of the tarn so hung above him as much in his mind as it was on the actual frame of the Earth the secrecy of that snowflake-coated scree slipping him sliding him down down into the valley's fold his knee jolting electrically.

Now he limped along the valley path towards the little barn and its five Scots pines. The snow was thickening quickly and squeaked beneath his steps. And the track he left in the grey-whiteness of this yielding substance was a repetition of one-clean boot-print-and-one-print-scuffed and this soft substance into which he divulged his injured trail was not yet hours old and after this night and another day would be melted gone. And the beck beside the path followed him and his deep tiredness effortlessly with its careless noise. He thought he could hear a voice in the water or was it remembering something she'd read to him? *This is where all The stars wear through This is where all The angels wear thread Bare their gowns of sky.* He wanted so much to be at the shelter now, he longed for the pines & the barn to grow out of darkness.

Then he was there pushing against the wood of the door his fingers fumbling the latch the door creaked as it opened. Then. Creaked as it was shut. Again. Immediately the snug quietness of the little place enveloped him. The dark white-flecked wind so far away and faint hissed peacefully through the pines outside. He slumped on to hay bales and let himself flop backwards. His headtorch picked out the cobwebbed beams and the backs of the thick slates keeping the sky away from him. He quickly slipped into an exhausted stupor, his mind emptying like a pool suddenly undammed. It was as if a part of his brain had fallen away from him. The ewe and all of that day already were gone far from him. He sank to sleep.

But then after a while of sleep's thick breathing the sweet scent of the hay pulled through his nose entered his memories and lit them. He sat up suddenly and thought of lush grass growing then cut and dried in sun. And then his shoulders trembled and a great shaking took hold of him and bursting sobs came out from his mouth as his eyes brimmed and his cheeks streamed and his nose dripped. A long shuddering wail flowed out from his throat. He knew he was weeping in a way he'd only ever witnessed once before. And that he'd forgotten long ago. He wept as once his mother had. As his small child-self sat on the trembling bed close to her stroking her huge warm hands.

Compass III

slow mountains pattern
the connected

places' spread

The Geology Section from
Stanage The Definitive Guide
also from   *Museum of The Stanage-ophone*

gritstone   compressed dense grey
1 or 2 notches of geological pressure beyond sandstone

300 million years ago
a bedding process laid down strata
from erosion of northern mountains
billions of tonnes of tiny mountain-bits were moved
by rivers   this wealth of fragments deposited
at deltas & mouths
later became our Pennines & Peak

sometimes submerged by sea
bedded in with layers of smashed shells

particles of grit compacted   bonded hard

then patient weather set to work
with its liquid chisel & file of air
and all the time on Earth

drag fingers across grit's surface
rough grips skin

black rubber + grit = high friction

in bright light the grey glints   star-specks
the grey is spattered with particles of quartzite
the grey when your nose is close to it comprises
many colours: subtle faints of greens & rusts

these colours can flare

bright through a vision of adrenaline

embedded in the ripples of rock are smooth
pebbles   and sometimes jagged
chips of quartz
algae-streaks & blooms
of lichen add layers
to the mosaic

zoom-out

the gritstone crag is architecture   gothic
& modernist mixed   abrupt blocks or intricate fins
(it is said 'God made rock to climb on'   and in Barcelona
Gaudi stole many of the designs)

slabs & rounded buttresses are decorated
with dark cracks & breaks   horizontal & vertical
some of the cracks are frosted at their rims
with climbers' chalk

and where the climbers' hands & feet've not scrubbed
sometimes grass or heather sprouts
from ledges or cracks
even slender rowans will push
their roots between the stone's seams

if left alone for long gritstone greens   peat creeps
back into the breaks   vegetation takes

but it wont be until humans cease
that Stanage Edge's vegetable flesh grows
again over its elegant bones   when its name

is a lost sound

that once came from the mouths
of animals called Homo sapiens

aeons ago

a 'Johnny Dawes' is a dot

a grey dragon of grit writhes distances
pixels of time colour stone
a resolution in a *kinetic museum* is immense
a resolution is never resolved
a 'Johnny Dawes' is a dot on a hard skin
a hard skin is dots
sand-dots compressed
a speed of geology leaves 'Johnny' standing still
a dot of time
a time leaves a 'Dawes' open

met   al on

                                        stone climbers

                clan   k kit muffled

all   oy peals krabs'

                                        clinking sna /
                                                    ps

Climber & Pedlar, Borrowdale, Autumn 2007

Each year that comes
the pedlar appears,
limping down through
Borrowdale [...]
                    – Irvine Hunt

Christopher Lichen clings,
as best he may, to a
suddenly slick
Shepherd's Crag.
Borrowdale's low
lascivious sky has dreamed
its rain and drenched
The Bludgeon.

The fat dark clouds scrape
across his head as the fresh
rain-fragrance rising
from the woods does some

thing to Chris's mind, or
perhaps to his world.

The rock becomes a faint
foil. It's a resonating
membrane be
tween times; a porous

divide. Christopher Lichen's face is in
this world, but his fingers feel
an other

side. His Wild

Country Friends are floppy blobs
of metallic dew. His Arc'teryx soft
-shell & North

Face base layer slip
off his skin like oil-slick. His

Edelrid ropes glow
like tungsten filaments.
And his belayer – she

is a cairn of bones
at the far
end of a vast

nylon umbilicus.

Chris, bless him, is sure his body
's about to fall.
That that dis

connecting of hu

man flesh from aeons-old
mineral is imminent. But

each of his breaths now
takes a ghost's hour.
So it is Chris is

nailed still for good

on an other Shepherd's
Crag of some
where else, made

of a shimmering soft
& humming stuff

other than stone.

And then there he
is: The Lakeland Pedlar,
limping down the vertical world,
his eager eyes fix
-ing Chris's. The Pedlar has
such a pale gaze. And listen:

The Pedlar's toes poking
from his rotten boots – how
sickly they squeak
on this other Shepherd
Crag's other-rock.

The Pedlar's hoping
for a sale. He's fresh
from a Borrowdale woods; but
a Borrowdale woods not
like ours. His Borrowdale is over

there way

to the left of eternity. Its shapes
& creatures whip
through us with
-out our knowing. But

our Chris Lichen, bless
him, he's feeling

elsewhere's all.

Now The Pedlar's very close
to Christopher Lichen's pinned
& aching frame. Chris can smell
the grass & bracken
The Pedlar's slept in; he can read

the paper lengths
of old news The Pedlar wrapped
around his legs when
he kipped in the pass.

Chris can feel
The Pedlar's breath near his ear.

So it is

The Pedlar speaks like breeze
through a gap
in a drystone wall,
and with syllables picked
out of 1907:

'Ay, right
you are Christopher Lichen
clad in your coloured
cloths & fangel kit. How
about you buy now
from me. Ay, I see

'you be a bit
surprised, for the passing
of a century has come

'again. How now
our bones ache together
for the sake

'& hiss of men's business.'

comfortingly rough grit grips
fingerprints as a climb's

                              shapes play

a person's skeleton with
a careless solidity old

                              as hills'

                              hands

from In Slate's Hands

also from the back leaves of
Ground Up's *Llanberis Slate*

for Ian Lloyd-Jones

this climber
has slate's gaze
a total of grey steadiness

he can see
the rainbow in slate's grey

his Welsh voice
cracks slate consonants
yet polishes with vowels

he speaks of new routes
& edgy slate grades

he has worked at play

slate has ripped & dusted
his Montane jacket
his pale grey hands wear
blood-black nicks

all day slate
has had his soul
attention

all day slate's family
has worked with him
his Grandfather's
flat slate ghost has

lived 3d through
his frame's movements

I cannot shake
his hand for fear
of slate's tons
& tiny razors

he has his
Grandfather's hands

slate hands

The Purest

Once having learned to climb, the gods' godliest trick was giving up.

The fine line, the narrow path, the thin
route, the technical, up
iced crag, the long
length of direct obsession, energy condensed,
one slick streak of precise motion, efficient

      bottom to top.

      All very well, but

Christopher Lichen had grander designs: he'd tie
all the lines, weave
a familiarity; a deep

      intercourse with the ground of one mountain.

The summit has its point, its pap, its view; it's
the bit where ground ends and sky begins, but
after years of wam-bam and numbered names
Christopher Lichen wanted to know

      the full extent:

His heart's heat must pulse
along the twists, re-entrants, arcs,
and flipbacks of every last
of one mountain's contours, in fact,
it might sound mad,
but Christopher Lichen's fingers must trace
the rugosities & angles of every

      one of one

mountain's boulders, pebbles & rocks, its cracks,
its scree cones; all must be learned –
soft cushions of moss, hard
gobs of solidified mist; he must sniff
out the list to the last ice
crystal. Light

        must be sifted

through thoughts so every last kiss
of photon on solid will've been felt.
And vibrations

of animal-mood must be shivered, racing
his skin's electrical impulses – the unseen
moments of every
insect, snail, bird, fox, fish, deer, & frog, all
to the last tiny mass that adds

        to one mountain's vast.

        So he started

at the obvious place – the mountain's base,
the foot-of, the where
the flat flees as ground rises
with a visual cry. Each

pitch a place measured
as a decade; he described
a kind of pious conical ascent. He threw
hoops of visualised travel; stacked

        pacts of concentric visits. So his memory

of motorways was erased
by his balance
and the picking
of pebbles
to make
no progress on. The trickle

of afternoon melt became

the dissolving
of knowledge-of
LED lights. The screech

of facsimiles & that blue
glow-bleed from screens went on

-&-on, but in others'

worlds without him, out

side his rugged intricate rings of
ground. A

round and around:

a man slower than an hour hand. A man alone.

As he circled choughs circled
in his ear; learned
to hover on the thermals of his thoughts.

That distant cache
of oxygen bottles, rattling
tent-fabric-&-poles,

cadavers, &
M&M's wrappers began

at last to not matter to this man.

Christopher Lichen's equipment & Gore-Tex gathered
moss & splodges of algae, greasy
& flaky green; his hair thickened
to gorse; his intestines blackened
into unread runes of peat as he ate
bits from under stones and from between
rock's joints; he became

the same

as the flowers that sprout from granite.

And by gods he knew
every millimetre
& inch-fraction of one mountain. But
only just learned
it all before his meat & bones began

the so so slow fall

into the mountain's ground. He soaked
into the pattern of tied

lines & the maze
of connected
places.

He spread. He died.

three mater
ials(')   un ar

range(d) pat
tern   feel

sky grits
tone grass

Figures

A gritstone crag is a kinetic museum.
                              – Johnny Dawes

Froggatt, Stanage, Birchen, Gardom's, Burbage, Curbar.

A gritstone edge is a crowd.   Characters

                of stone stood
                side by side all moving
                through centuries

with the immense unfathomable speed of

                                                    stillness

Each rock climb,
pictured and described in the guide,
is now a skeleton fleshed

with climbers' motion,   or the desire for motion.

                        .

hands' geo   evolution being

                        sun in mist grit's

                                            is
                                            is is

tip

toed on
a rip

ple of grit

stone fin
gers feel

ing to st
ick to

geol

ogy's rim
a moor

going on go
ing on o

ver horiz

ons

Perceptions West
of Outer Edge,
A Peak District
(a 1926 or a 2013)

if you approach
Crow Stones from

just a right angle

in a right light
in a kindest of

fast ragged air

one stone
will perch whilst

its feathers
ruffle and

blacken so
some form

of you will
hear or

will've heard

grit scrape
as crow's *caw*

                                        if you

                              approach the
                              stones on the

                        wrong day when the

                                light is swerving
                                         and the

                                        air rubs
                                   like warm

                        tweed across cheeks

                                   i will not
                              know a stone

                              as difference as
                                 tiny in near

                              distance where

                              one man caught
                              miniature in four

                        postures helps versions

                                   of him or
                                 her self to

                              ascend some
                    b
              roken e
                      roded b
                          ust

Craig

from The Life & Climbs of Craig

flowing burning
muscles past
rock prophecies

Two Legends

I

Rock was without touch
Rock the of-Earth
Until an idea

of Craig gleamed
in a quartz eye

Rock was then the heart
Rock like liver, rock for lungs
Unable then to repel touch
Rock the blood flowing solid
Rock the guts burning Earth's fuels
Rock also the muscles
Striving to pull past the first crux
Rock the nerves, rock the brain
With its stone prophecies
Rock also the soul, the huge hammer
        of the cry that, crashing, could utter
With the tongue's piton

II

Rock is the human's head sweating
Rock is the black pebble gazing from a socket
Rock is the clot flopped from the wound of Earth

Rock is the world-bone, just poking through
An egg of rock
Where feet & fingers alternate their pressures

To hatch a man, a rock rainbow
Bent through friction
                              through oblivion
But climbing

Lineage

In the beginning was Gravity
Who begat Terror
Who begat Skin
Who begat Friction
Who begat Tendon
Who begat Nylon
Who begat Gogarth
Who begat Protein
Who begat Sweat
Who begat Stanage
Who begat Adam
Who begat Ligament
Who begat Mary
Who begat Rock
Who begat Now
Now Now Now

Who begat Craig

Screaming, for friction &
Writhing grubs of tendons, crusts

All Rock's offerings

Craig

Trembling unclothed in Rock's raw palm

Examination at the Crux-Door

Who owns these scrawny fingers? *Rock.*
Who owns these darting-for-holds eyes? *Rock.*
Who owns these high-air lungs? *Rock.*
Who owns this jacket of ligaments? *Rock.*
Who owns these unsayable brains? *Rock.*
All this hive of flesh? *Rock.*
This stone-stuck face? *Rock.*
These blind but tender toes? *Rock.*
These shallows of now deep as Earth? *Rock.*

Given, released, or held pending Gravity?
Held.

Who owns the whole of the vertical Earth? *Rock.*
Who owns all motion? *Rock.*

Who is stronger than despair? *Rock.*
Who is stronger than agony? *Rock.*
Stronger than love? *Rock.*
Stronger than death? *Rock.*
But who is stronger than Rock?
                                    Obsession, evidently.

Pass, Craig.

Craig Tries the Media

he wanted to wax
songful about rock

he wanted no comparisons
with worlds or anything to do
with worlds'

oversold rubber
he didn't even want a tongue

tongues waggling online
with their forked clicks

he wanted to climb songful
very clear

but this territory
with its borders
was jammed on his hand
and his throat was clipped
between The President's
thumb & index finger
whilst in person
The Joker held the blood-loop
of his rope so

he tried solo
but oligarchs flogged his tendons

so he beasted himself
and escaped across fields filled with
mines & razor-wire he fled

across wastes in his head as
his body bled in a
gym in Sheffield

then he tried again
again he tried solo

he shucked his hi-tech husk
he got so naked when
he touched rock it hurt

he simply wanted
to climb simply
songful

but still
London's Shard gripped one wrist whilst
Google's servers gripped the other

he stared into rock's quartz eye
his tongue moved like
China's Yellow River

he touched rock's smiles
his voice rubbed like some billions

of fingers wearing away keyboards

he gripped whilst
for the time

being rock's surface

held

                                    tiptoed
                                    on a ripple

                                    of gritstone

                                    fingers feeling
                                    to stick to

adren   geology's rim
aline's cr
                                    a moor going

isp flow lets
                                              on

light s
eep from   going on

gritstone's deep   over horizons
shape-change voy

age cryst

als blink as
stone pro

ceeds

Key Ping Ba(p)la(n)ce

I was sitting on a ledge high up on a crag called Clogwyn y
Ddysgl. Below me the small watery letterbox-slot of Llyn Bach
invited me to post silly messages ... not exactly in the same way
Plath's Wuthering Heights sheep did with their black slots. This
slot glittered, and I was elated, so obviously the invitation to
post was also one to celebrate ... in that moment I felt – being
that absurdly over-the-top personhood known as poet – that I
could sing a psalm to Earth's centre, to praise the weak but very
beautiful force of gravity. Fortunately, I quickly came back to the
matter, the rock, in hand and focused again on the practicalities
of climbing. My climbing partner – a tough, practical and yet
gentle & pragmatic woman – was much relieved, to say the least.
And to say 'the least' is very hard for a poet to do.

> The   sheep   know   they   are,
>   sing   their   dirty   clouds,
> Grey   weather.
> The   lack   lots   of   their   pupils   take   me   .
> It   is   being   into   space,
> A thin, ill   sage.

I was once told by a sheep, as I balanced along the knife-edge
crest of a boulder, only nine feet high, mind, but nevertheless,
I was told by a sheep that poets are absurd, dangerously absurd.
High-minded approaches to the stuff of stone and the weak but
cunning force of gravity quickly go awry. And even the most
rational of people can find themselves being told off by the
utterly resilient woollen beings that wander much of Britain's
uplands, if such persons approach the zone with high minds. Of
course finding one's self is far easier than losing it. As voters know
too well! As for poets, well ... being balanced on-&-along a line,
knowing when to end it, the line that is, counts for much. Each
step has to be counted, and counted on. One step at a time, and
soon, you have a whole collection of steps.

Friction, momentum, gravity. If the poet engages with these three through impeccable tenacity, as well as gentle negotiation, then the poet can fling off 'the' and become 'a'. To be 'a' teetering on an edge shows how very fragile & maskly 'the' really is. I, or an I, marvels at what an I has learned about gravity and how bundled attentions of flesh called muscles-&-ligaments-&-tendons – held on a stone frame we call bones – can become an aerial. When we sing we sway, and sway is dance. So, there I am on this ledge staring down at a dark yet glistening slot of water, and I am listening to gravity sing. And do you know what, I very nearly thought of spreading my wings, but was put off by how pointless climbing would become if I had in a reality done so. I mean if I'd really flown, rather than just really thought about it. Often climbers can be very arrogant, it goes with(out) the territory: the vertical expanse that maps forget. However, the arrogance of poets completely outstrips that of climbers ... to believe that the vibration made in one's throat can really keep a being in place on a line between abyss & existence is absurd self-indulgence second only to that of the gods'.

However, give me a break, or a gap, or a crevasse or caesura ... can you not read how I'm making some effort at humility? My title has wilfully refused 'my', because the notion of 'keeping' balance is daft enough without adding to it the notion that I, me, a selfhood, might 'own' balance.

It was when A raven at the top of Tryfan's South Summit said to me, "Watch Your Step" ... it was just then-right-now that I knew Offkilter was Is's swooping. And I was literally covered in flying ants. Still, I stayed in balance, momentarily at home in a house of balance, and came down from the mountain ... not mad ... but not a poet either. I came down as a person who had been touched by gravity.

not earth's pull
earth's push

he hadn't realised
the gravity

of the situation

all along all
the while a

line

of the dist
ant hills

sunlight's writing

suddenly he got

it like
glee

or

guilt

As I Cramponed Up One Morning

(whilst being guided by W.H. Auden)

As I cramponed up one morning,
   climbing up Distant Peak,
the fields upon the far-off plains
   were crowds of starved meek.

And upon the smile of a curling cornice
   I heard the weather sing
a loud chill to the depths of lava:
   'Love has no meaning.

'I'll be random, I'll be random
   as every flake of pain,
the crystals of no meaning
   will fall and will remain,

'the serac is just white blood
   stiff at the vulva of death,
and the avalanche is the last slide
   of male cells bereft.'

Then all the warm in the atoms
   began to weep and spume:
a tongue of ions lit the skies
   while the mountains grew maroon.

Rock-purple shadows coagulated
   as men in pin-striped suits
cramponed up rock-hard accounts,
   and snowfields glazed with loot.

The hot breath of granite entwined
    with the soft, red pulse of flesh,
while oxygenless lungs gasped
    hollowed-out children's deaths.

The pin-stripes wriggled lasciviously
    on Chomolungma's teat,
the monk in the ice-grotto died,
    and the dust devoured the wheat.

'I'll be random, I'll be random,'
    the snowflake laughed its fractals,
'Go on, chalk the cloth of the mountains

    with   lines   of   lifts   to   hotels,

'and I will break the fingery dance
    and the climber's brilliant show.
Your money may be green in your wallet
    but not in The Abode of Snow.

'Your cupboard stinks in the glacier,
    your bed-stains show in the desert,
and cracks in icy snouts snot out
    your ancestors' flattened hearts.

'O stare, stare at the spectre
    that waves from rainbowed clouds;
wonder at the cost of his ice-axe:
    how light, and stiff, and proud!

'O climb, climb in the wilderness
    as naked as genuine grief,
and you will reap the roots of id
    but still be born of thieves.'

It was late, late in the evening,
    as I climbed down Distant Peak;
the loose stuffing from my armchair
    was snow around my feet.

And the media talked of wars and mountains;
    of how many deaths today,
while the random fractals kept falling:
    sugary and heavy on névé.

2003

a first boot
print on high

hill sends

valley ref   lections
wobbling miles

Zeal
for Nick

down
in a

valley a

key

board waits
for s   ore

fingertips   as

a raw
voice

grows

gentle

on   an

.

e d g e

The Tale of The Journey
to The Dead Engine in The Shed
at The Bottom of Heaven's Walls
for Johnny

On the slate shelf
the slate-backed book

see the slatey pages open

—

Once upon a distance
near near ago three

characters began
and began

a trip to the depths
of Slate's

Quarry near Dinorwig

the three's names
scratched on a leaf of slate

      Ony . Iky . Ark

all followers each
along their way of

a fancy slatey dragon's
trailing rattling tale

—

Ony led
snakily along levels
and down ladders

Ark said slate
and felt
slate's sounds
smooth & sharp
through his mouth
and Ark engraved
on slate's wafer flakes
slate's words
with slate's
brittle tongue

Iky clicked her eye
and took slate's
shapely colours
as keepsakes
on membranes
grey's rainbows
& slate's sights
framed for eyes

Ony danced
with & on
slate's shapes

Ony's body
fitted to slate's lips
simply like tiles
& rain

Ony was
slate's nimble limbs

Ony stretched
soft flesh across
slate's solidity and

stretched slate's

fluid through
fixed flesh

—

Now follow the slivers
the little slatey prints

the thin tick-ticks
of slate-time unsli   cing

don't be late don't be late
for old Slate

& Slate's chapters &

keep

sakes

—

bus stop quarry car park

the graceful furniture of fence-jumping goats

walking between the barbed-wire

the quarryman eating salad at watford gap

riding slate's incline

the groundless train=track (traintrack traint   rack)

the slate scree-stack & slate artichokes

slate's Stalker & telegraph-pole-crucifix

along the level beyond lost world

the moss-coated slate gangplank & sheepy cross-bones

chat with a rowan on the edge of slate's abyss

the dizzy view of the shed & the pool

down the rust-red thready ladders

the wet level & the dry

into the garden

Ony draws his line on a slice of slate

the shed & the dead engine

the seam of sound (hydro O(h)m)

—

Of course they all lived ... so

watch the sl   ate book

cli   ck

sh   ut

rocky e   cho
ech

o sin   ging sing

ing faint
er fain

ter fey a
cross nar

cissus's
mirr

or

Compass IV

a head

in stone tri
angulation

a woke

(M)a(p)sk

my legend is
on skin

bone co
ded below

I'm an
I on

an I in
an I as

mate
rial
in ti

me's s
pace

◩

let land glance   let land glance at its selves
(at)   let land glance at   selves
(its)   selves   let land glance   its selves

put a paper mirror up   let land lance   selves

let ground gaze deep down   let land   at its selves
into unlit solidity under

                                   let and glance at   selves

in to un   let land   elves

lit sol
id

ity un
der er er

a

very well
made face

let an echo
fasten fast

still & quick
to a survey

(one of ordnance) of

Narcissus's
ordinary skull

◪

practising me nav
pacing bearings

staring at paper
my leg ends

pressing real feat
ures below the

water-tight sheet
of map in its plastic

a world all gone
symbolic &

virtually three
d contoured &   contorted counted courted caught court

coloured accordingly
coloured metaphorically
coloured allegorically
coloured mythologically
coloured scientifically
coloured empirically
coloured imaginatively

well

an exclamation
an expression
in a sentence

represented
as a blue
w on paper

butt

a deep wet
connection down
down down
through ground

well

my frown on my
map as I paced
my mountain

it was or is
or will

be a papery crease
my my   my eyes

were ringed by
brown-orange lines

at not ten
but five-&-sum

-times nine
metre intervals

I could feel the cool

wet plastic of the map
case pressed to my

nose i
          (follow(ed))

wore I wear
i will
wear a square

mask

I had a gridded
i have a gridded I will
have a grId   ded

face

◩

o o OS so
imagine my

dismay as I
did do & will
say

as i placed
a my's finger
tips to a my's

face scape
I traced

a textured surface
my stubble shrubs
or perhaps long
grasses or an exp

anse of for   estry

imagine

my dismay
as even (as un
even)

even as feet paced
and fingers felt
a face's textures an

i could not
feel below
an am's
malleable
soft

ness any bones

frameless phantom
an I an am

soundless ground
each well a sliced
disc of flat blue all

's well that
ends (s)well well

well very
well then

any rock gone
or faint as

some old
song sucked

away on wind

An End of An Affair

Since the age of ten I've had an intimate relationship with Ordnance Survey 1:25 000 maps. Recently, that relationship, one of desire and trust rooted in imaginative and perceived landscapes, has been put under considerable strain. I suppose 'desire' & 'trust' were never going to make good bedfellows in the first place, and I now know that I was being fooled, or perhaps it was even I who was doing the fooling.

As a young map-reader I fell in love; fell into imagined landscapes. And I trusted that what was being represented on paper was what I was walking on and amongst. Over the years, getting to know Ordrey better, I've come to realise (or is that imagine?) that like any identity, she (or he?) was far more complex & secretive than I had first assumed. But, there was consistency: Ordrey's surface (in places pretty & delicate and in others incisive & masculine) always displayed layered fields of depth on one plane utilising **constant symbols**. You knew where you were with Ordrey, or at least the Ordrey I used to know.

Before I go on to divulge my grievance, to set down my complaint utilising alphabetic symbolism, before I finally crystallise my loss, I hope the reader, the wanderer, will indulge my reminiscing just one more time.

The connection between poetry & maps is almost obvious, because it is 'natural' to metaphorical minds. There has been much written and spoken about this link to the 'almost obvious', to the 'hidden unhidden'. For example, the French-Welsh postmodern poet-philosopher Gene Llaudribard has written extensively on the subject in *The Cat A Kitten Copied* (*Le Chat un Chaton Copiés*, Llanberis, 1969); perhaps her most famous, and possibly over-quoted epigram goes thus: *Simulation n'est pas différente de la simulation; c'est exactement la même chose comme quelque chose de différent. (Simulation is no different to simulation; it is exactly the same as anything different.)* Poems & maps are the same things and are as different to each other as the differences they represent. Ordrey's version of Snowden *is* Snowden (o yes it is!) despite actually being the (a) Snowden that is only as high as the thickness of the paper Ordnance Survey choose to print upon (plus the thickness of the ink!).

But I digress, as it so easy to do when pouring [sic] over a map (rain has to be taken account of in British uplands) – one can be one minute planning a walk in mountainous country, paying close attention to timing and height gained, to measuring bearings to walk along should the weather become inclement, and then suddenly in the next minute, without one even realising it (knowing it, perceiving it?), one is pondering the imagined presence of an old quarry one has never visited before, but has suddenly noticed as **a pretty frill of craggy black ink**. So, I will cease my digression, I will return to my promised reminiscence, to one of the good times Ordrey & I shared, that we created together, before things (possibly real things) turned sour.

Mountainous country changes rapidly, depending on the season or the weather. Paths can be washed away, or they can be shrouded in mist or darkness. So, how beautiful to enter a realm of special presence with Ordrey – one of pacing along bearings whilst noting one's walking speed according to Naismith, whilst determining aspects of slopes, and all whilst not caring that one could not see where one was going, due to fog or darkness or even both. There was never any groping with Ordrey, everything was done through skilful grace. Just like that time in my early twenties, descending from Fairfield, in the English Lake District, one inclement April night:

Do you remember, Ordrey, how you held my hand all that dark, windy wet descent? And do you remember what reassured me the most? Yes, it was the ground, the very ground you imagined on paper and I felt beneath my feet. Each step. And yes, you know how stable a foundation the ground is, how deep it goes below all of us. And Ordrey, what is it that builds such deep foundation? Yes, Ordrey, yes – it is bedrock! And you remember how we both loved the outcrops, the crags, the architecture of rock exposed to the sky, the bones of a world poking through its skin ... Ordrey, it was always so thick and blackly printed upon *your* skin, the crags would stand out in an instant of gazing upon *you*, they would not hide. They would not hide!

And so to my complaint. When I first met Ordnance Survey 1:25 000 maps (back in the 20th Century) the rock features were clearly printed in solid black ink, but since around 2009/2010 these features have been faded. Crags are now faintly represented through dot-matrix grey-scale. I am at a loss.

Dear Ramblers,

I'm crags distinct
that visibility way

terrain endowed

the rescued
perceived-of

•

for using marks
in poor rights of

dangerous far

distinct way
endowed
rescued of
marks of
far matter

be

a

features carefully matter

•

I'm that terrain
the perceived

for in danger
be a feature

less suspect that

out

to

by

I would be very grateful if you could give me your carefully considered and expert opinion on this matter

I'm rather dismayed to see that OS have faded out their symbols for crags. The rock features on their 1:25 maps used to be printed using distinct solid black ink - they are now very faint dot-matrix marks that are very hard to discern in good light, never mind in poor visibility. The present maps now give the impression that rights of way can be easily and clearly followed across tricky and dangerous terrain, as on first glance rugged rugged hillsides now appear to be far less endowed with rock. I am very concerned about this, as I suspect that the growing incidence of inexperienced 'walkers' having to be rescued by the Mountain Rescue services is exacerbated by a perceived ease of access to upland country, caused by this fading out of crag features.

terrain
perceived
danger
feature

I'm rather dismayed to see that OS have faded out their symbols for crags. The rock features on their 1:25 maps used to be printed using distinct solid black ink - they are now very faint dot-matrix marks that are very hard to discern in good light, never mind in poor visibility. The present maps now give the impression that rights of way can be easily and clearly followed across tricky and dangerous terrain, as on first glance rugged hillsides now appear to be far less endowed with rock. I am very concerned about this, as I suspect that the growing incidence of inexperienced 'walkers' having to be rescued by the Mountain Rescue services is exacerbated by a perceived ease of access to upland country, caused by this fading out of crag features.

I would be very grateful if you could give me your carefully considered and expert opinion on this matter.

symbols printed
matrix mind

impression across
hillsides concerned

'walkers' exacerbated by

[blank]

care fully matter

•

dismayed rock solid
hard present
easily first rock incidence
mountain of features be
considered

printed mind across
concerned by
matter

across by matter

•

see features' ink
to present and

glance rock
growing by
perceived crag

present be considered

ink & rock by crag

•

OS 1:25
no(w) go(o)d (n)ow
followed rugged

solid present
incidence be
considered

•

faded maps
very light

I would be very grateful if you could give me your carefully considered and expert opinion on this matter.

I'm rather dismayed to see that OS have faded out their symbols for crags. The rock features on their 1:25 maps used to be printed using matrix marks that are very hard to discern now give the impression that rights of way can be tricky and dangerous terrain, as on first endowed with rock. I am very concerned about this, as I suspect that the growing be rescued by the Mountain Rescue country, caused by this fading out of crag features.

distinct solid black ink – they are now very faint dot-in good light, new mind in poor visibility. The present maps easily and clearly followed across glance rugged hillsides now appear to be far less incidence of inexperienced 'walkers' being to services is exacerbated by a perceived lack of access to upland

give followed
hillsides

services country
features grateful expert

•

out-used faint
never impression
· across now
about having by
fading

•

I'm **rather** dismayed to see that OS have faded **out** their **symbols** for crags. The **rock** features on their 1:25 maps **used** to **be** printed using distinct **black** ink – they are now very **faint** dot-**matrix** marks that are very **hard** to discern in **good** light, **never** mind in poor **visibility**. The **present** maps now **give** the **impression** that rights of way **can** be easily and **clearly** followed across **tricky** and **dangerous** terrain, as **on** first glance **rugged** hillsides **now** appear to **be far** less endowed   with **rock**. I am very concerned **about** this,   faint impression   as I **suspect** that the **growing** incidence **of** inexperienced '**walkers**' having to   **be** rescued by **the** Mountain **Rescue**   services is exacerbated **by** a perceived **ease**   now by fading   of access to upland country, caused **by**   this fading out of crag **features**.

I **would** be very **grateful** if you **could** give me your carefully considered and **expert** opinion on **this** **matter**.

followed hill side's country   expert

About Fields

My dearest Odrey,

Now that you ask ... It is also to do with the various surfaces in that particular area of The Peak District and how they slip over each other in our imaginations, and how a mappish mentality, or the head-space one gets into when navigating using paper, hints at depths through flatness. Contour lines being a case in point, 3d rendered 2d. There's also a lot to do with vertical & horizontal, for example a climber's journey can be zero metres across a map but a number of metres upwards. Numbers & counting. And as a matter of course, of course so often co-ordinates are one way of pin-pointing, but in being only one way often leave a navigator oblivious of other 'dimensions' or tracks. Surely you see that?! Climbers focus on the absolute minute touchableness of a landscape/cragscape, whereas most walkers don't actually touch with the actual skin of their feet, and tend to travel along or through, rather than mostly up. And a shepherd some hundreds of years ago at some time travelled through or rather stayed in that particular landscape in a very different way that is hard(er) to imagine. To navigate with an accurate map and use numbers, heights, bearings or pacing gives one a great deal of comfort, especially when the weather is not so good. But to think about how it would be, for one used to navigating from paper, to find themselves suddenly on the moor mapless is rather scary. Although some would claim that The United States' God Pointer Star trumps all roadmaps to the future, not to say utterly supersedes paper in the digital earera. But forgive me, I degress ... or was that degrees? ... or perhaps just regress? ... or even dead grass? ... where was I? ... ah yes, the moors, the moors. Well, moors *are* scary. They tend to be more towards the convex rather than the nestling concave of the valley, that a farmer can easily survey. Perhaps not so much mystery in a valley, or at least not in that scary way when one is surrounded by horizons that roll away from you down convex places. So, I guess a field system, the system being important, is actually another kind of map, be it a lifesized map. People find fields comforting. Although long fields in Wales do tend to cause a sweet angst or bitter glee about misplacement ... rather like an old map of somewhere familiar, now hard to read because of the wear & tear caused by distance rubbing it. But yes, another kind of map – that's all I meant. I don't know why my words hurt you. It was only to do with the fact (or perhaps f(r)iction) that a dry stone wall disappearing beyond the convex is a hand rail to take you somewhere and yet at the same time a bound ary to confine you ... you can't see where it goes but you know a human put it there. Is it the 'human' thing that got at you? And then I sup pose there is that obvious pun on more and moor, but it is actually rather serious in bad weather, and certain shapes that can be learned, i.e. fields make less of the moor. Perhaps the shepherd's instinct to count his or her sheep in the valley, using numbers, is put up on the moors, expressed in the form of fields. Each field will have or would've had a name, or perhaps a number. You know of course that my dad's fields all had names, but were mostly referred to by their numbers when talking to the farm workers. Field 1 was near the farmhouse, the higher numbered fields further away. And they still are to this day. So numbers can control distance, or at least make humans think they can control distance. I'm sorry if you misread me. Any way ...

That's a bit of a sprawl of thoughts, but I hope it helps. Or did you need more? Or do you know more than you are letting on?

Regards and fond degrees, a Mark on a map

Black Crag Grey

some thing un
uttered up

there on Fairfield but
something of si

lent solidity re
assuring

> *Because we must also give* [/]
> *an exterior destiny to the interior being.*

alone I wandered across rock
y high ground whilst Lakeland pulled

thick shadows down
into her hollows
its hollows (it's hollows)
his hollows

a last black
bird deep in a dale
below glugs
out a last liquid f(r)iction
from a tipped
up jug of himself a

whiff of song suddenly
here (from there) then

gone

Lakeland's blanket spread rucked
over hiding children over

childlike bones of rock

miles & miles of undulating so
lidity darkening

kilometres & kilometres

miles darkening kilometres

of flat sheet deep
as poetry as

as as   as   as   as   as odd as
                                             England the light

fades fast as I looked
at my map I'd intended

to be benighted I felt
my aloneness fade
to cloud crowds of
crags crags blackening as

felt fade of blackening sun

sun sank* gathered   *[s   inks]

round the phosphorescing bezel of my compass
(flaring yellow as daffodil-neon in my head   torch's glow)

> *Each one of us, then, should speak* [/]
> *up his roads, his crossroads, h*[er] [/]
> *roadside benches* [...]

an army of cartographers long
dead bled out from the crags' blackness

[...]   *each one of us should make* [/]
a surveyor's map of his [/her] *lost* [/]
fields [&] *meadows.*

ordnance rattled the ground
and a great rambling military being began   begins
plans some
  one up ahead jokingly calls   her Ordrey

the map in my hand (head?) – Ordrey
I in the hand of my map I
crawling across Ordrey's vast lap
(Ordrey's mind or mine?)
  (Ordrey's mine or mind)

        some one up ahead made (makes)
        a gravestone in sea
        through stone shaped as
        a triangulation pillar incised with an in
        scription I awoke (will wake) to a past
        future joke:

Ordrey Nancy Surefey RIP

                    I
                 I asked
m a p h a n d a   I ask my   c r os s m i n d
              I asked my map
              I asked my map to
           I ask my map to be
           I asked my map to be my
           I asked my map to be my mask
                                    map asked
s o m e g r a v e s t o n e t h r o u g h t r i a n g u l a t i o n I j o k e
                                    map as mask
                                      ma(p)sk

I must

've grimaced through
ten metre vertical inter   vals with
an attitude of altitude I
must've frowned a   grid I
                                                        gr
                                                        id

must've widened my eyes in
to two tarns surprised in two re
-entrants of my skull   (i)

F   air   field's ground was a
round me and

                    I was a
                    round a
                    ground of a
                    map but

                    my rock my
                    ground my
                    crags were
                    massive sol
                    id & black &
                    so de

                    spite mist
                    & night I

                                        was still

                                                        un

afraid a way a
head display(s)(ed)
lines & planes in
my mind's land

i round ground map my ground crags' massive id so spite & afraid head & mind's ghyll now bend-sends when marks written amongst footpaths rip clear as ghyll water (but(t))

I know now refraction
& plans bend so

opaque sends clear
signals when 'see

-through' marks rights
of way ways written
evaporate amongst hosts
of eroding footpaths

green rip-

here here here here here her here here here her here here

here dashes streaking

Law's trace across
paper landscapes
(trouncing daffs (&
besides the trees are
beneath the lakes))

I read
written as written
read(s) me

Ordrey RIP
reality in print

here Law's paper troun   cing
besides beneath
cissus's
flat mirr
or
ter fey a
cross nar
ing faint
er fain
o singing sing
rocky echo
ech

native

Ordrey
never ordinary all
ways muscular as
ordnance yet
pretty as a colour
ful legend

I knew from the moment it began that my walk wasn't ordinary.

myth's mirth myth's   my 'the'
miss   spelled c   raft yes

mist emits   mist mist mist aches

I laugh I'm glad for a
joke-ghost a cart   o   graphical
phan   tom a comical navi   gator a placer
of flat vagi   nation

                    to keep to

                keep me

company she (or
he?) held

holds   my hand the same
hand that held   h olds

my map in its water   weeping outcrop so
tight case

*Something happened during my walk that marked it
in a way that I could not bear to see afterwards.*

one does not expect to meet Coleridge weeping
he's kneeling on a little outcrop
all the rock soaked & salty so
I glanced at Ordrey's thoughts
her lingering in reality a lingerie of symbolic shapes

my map's legend suddenly held a stain

a faint blurred bird
amazedly I gaze at this gray mark as its ink thickened in
to the unmist   akable gray   ceful shape of a flying al   bat   ross

I no longer have a copy of the Ordnance Survey Map

Coldridge said nothing which is unlike
him to say
the least but I smelled

his poetry & grief I
smell his worth

in words his un

saids printed in
fading vapours

But for [sometime] *I kept* [/]
the map. Destroying it seemed
like a guilty act, as if [...]

one does not expect
to meet rock as gloss
imagine my anguish   as
I suddenly discover   all

un like say
smell   i
worth un in
v a p o u r s

thoughts' shapes stain

kept
seemed
IF
expect
gloss

161

of Lakeland's
frame's made

of glass but no
not even glossy
glass a glass
shineless a matt
glass and
worse still or
worse in motion
not glass but

a jelly a

transparent wobbly

Lakeland's frames imagine ylneddus

stuff an
exudate of
distance some
anti-matter e
ven gaseous

crags suddenly ectoplasmic ecstasy
forgotten material remembered as

grey mist crags
as mist mist

ecstasy-remembered crags' mist in hollow grey of substance

holding
up a whole
mountain Fair

field a fade-in
flated hollow skinned
by some grey-fake
memory of

sub/   stance

                                        it is not easy to describe
            the exact mo

                        ment & posit

            ion

Where-When's felt rock
solid one
                        moment & then

                                                gone
Ordrey was truly lovely
the moon didn't come
out but had it done so I'm
sure her bones would've glowed   when's one
                                                     was moon
                                                    had bone's
through her frail gown   grail frown
                                                    frail glow a
                                                   swirling min
my bones glow below my Gore-Tex   iature other
an I of a me a
vortex of swirling symbols printed   gone gone o
invisibly-miniature along the life   nly whispers
                                                   sniff whispers

line on an other-than-mine palm   whispers' reader

gone one's gone ground that's
me: gone

                                        one only

only Ordrey's faint grey
whispers now

sniff sniff her last
whispers whilst

her last whispers last yes

one moon-bone's a
miniature o ther o

      er re   ader-dear here listen that

faint

        scent of

rock melted and

stretched on

wind reach

out and

Gloss as Rockery

This rockery is for those who do not know about climbing & mountain navigation as well as for those who do. Many of this rockery's definitions will be redundant for most climbers & mountain navigators.

The author is aware that this rockery is unlikely to be exhaustive, but could very well be exhausting. Please do, before venturing forward, ensure that you have with you the right equipment and that you are fully proficient in regard to its use. The surface of the rockery can at times be extremely uneven.

First epigraph: Gray Signer, an avatar of the author, or possibly *the* avatar of *an* author. (The author finally concedes that his obsession with the little words *a, an, and,* & *the* could very well in the end be the (a!) death of him.)
Second epigraph: Johnny Dawes, spoken to Mark Goodwin, very early on in the 21st Century.
Third epigraph: Ted Hughes.
Fourth epigraph: Menlove Edwards.

A Climber is Dialling Stone: *Stanage Edge* is one of the world's greatest rock-climbing venues, a few miles south-west of Sheffield. This miles-long edge expresses climb after climb through the glorious archi-texture of a rock known as *gritstone*.

    A Climber is Dialling Stone draws much from Peter Redgrove's sea poem *Abyssophone*, which ends with:

> *I seek out and dial again –*
>
> *Home's new number*
> *On the shellyphone; I dial British Seacom.*

Bored as a Boy on a Beach: Yosemite Valley, located in California's western Sierra Nevada mountains, is one of the most popular tourist spots on planet Earth. It is also 'home' to some of the world's longest immaculate granite rock routes, many of which require the climber to sleep out, and haul along with them their supplies & 'camping' kit, if not their 'belongings'! Such routes are akin to sea-voyages ... and the vertiginous history of the exploration of vast cliffs such as Half Dome & El Capitan, in some ways can be likened to the horizontal pioneering of the Wild West (but without the same level of violence).

Throughout, **Metaphysical Mountaineer** references Samuel Taylor Coleridge's work and moments in his life, and draws much from Richard Holmes' double-volume biography of Coleridge: *Early Visions* & *Darker Reflections*.

A Seagull's Shadow: *Lizard* refers to an area of Cornwall. Much of the rock type on The Lizard is known as *Serpentine*.

A Ghost Jokes: John Menlove Edwards was the most prolific of the British 1930s rock-climbing pioneers, and possibly the finest British climber before the Second World War. During the 30s he led many of the hardest routes wearing hobnailed boots. Mountaineer Geoffrey Winthrop Young described Menlove's climbing style thus: *Serpentine and as powerful as an anaconda coiling up loose or wet overhangs, I had the conviction that human adhesiveness in movement could go no further.* He was also essential to the evolution of rock-climbing guidebooks – starting a series of *Guides to the British Hills.* He likened his painstaking method of producing crag- & route-description to sweeping a cliff's surfaces with a searchlight. Menlove was a gifted, imaginative & idiosyncratic prose writer, and a poet. His poignant, literary writing about climbing is considered to be essential, and is of high quality. He was a progressive, clinical child psychiatrist, and also contributed to the foundation of the NHS. Menlove's life was beset with emotional difficulty. He was gay – throughout 1930s/40s/50s Britain! – and yet courageously tried to defend the human validity of homosexuality. During the Second World War he was a conscientious objector, and for a year during the war, Menlove removed himself from society to a small remote North Welsh cottage called Hafod Owen (a mile from any road). Here he lived alone ascetically and studied to advance his own new psychiatric theory, of which no documentation remains. He was ostracised by his professional peers. Finally, in 1958 he was overtaken by despair, and took his own life. Menlove said of himself: *I grew up exuberant in body but with a nervy, craving mind. It was wanting something more, something tangible. It sought for reality intensely, always as if it were not there... But you see at once what I do. I climb.* [For further reading see Jim Perrin's *Menlove*, and online: *A Black Rainbow: The Life and Times of Menlove Edwards* – footlesscrow.blogspot.com.]

Munro by Gone: *crampons* are spiked metal frames attached to mountain boots, designed to allow traction on ice & hard snow.

Adeptitude: *The Plantation* is a mixed woodland that includes some very distinguished beech trees. It is just below and part-way along Stanage Edge. This area is also considered to be one of the very best bouldering venues. Bouldering is a kind of rope-less climbing that concentrates on the gymnastics & dance of rock-movement, focused onto/into the small space/surface provided by a diminutive boulder. Rather than cliff- or crag-size jaunts or voyages, boulder-problems are a kind of free-verse Tai Chi of still-place intensity ...

Special Lighting, E2 5c †: This fiction obviously refers directly to Menlove Edwards, but it also references closely areas of his creative writing & guidebook writing. Menlove's fiction was profound & powerfully imaginative, as was some of his poetry. Examples of Menlove's poetry & fiction – including *End of a Climb*, *Scenery for a Murder*, & *The Climbers* – are appended to Jim Perrin's biography, *Menlove*.

Joanna Croston on *Special Lighting*: [...] *it sings along, up and down, side to side, back to reality off to dreamland and back again.*

The title – *Special Lighting, E2 5c †* – is the name & grade of a fictional climb, given as it might appear in a guidebook. Most climbing grades do not include the dagger symbol, which *indicates a route where the guidebook team may have doubt about some aspect of the route, such as being unsure of the line, or having an unconfirmed grade due to insufficient repeats. It is not meant to cast doubt on a first ascent* [from *Stanage, The Definitive Guide*].

A *sandbag* is a climb that is under-graded, and therefore much harder than it 'pretends' to be. To be *sandbagged* is to find one's self unpleasantly surprised on such an under-graded climb. To *sandbag* is to wilfully direct someone towards such an under-graded climb; or to deceive them about the correctly given grade of a climb, by making out that the route is at a lower grade. To wilfully downgrade one's own first ascent can sometimes also be an act of *sandbagging*, although such downgrading can also be due to modesty (rare in male climbers). The invented expression *sandbagging-bastard* is particular to the narrator of this story. Apparently, *to sandbag* is of 19th century origin, and describes the act of bludgeoning someone with a small, sand-filled bag prior to robbing them. The verb has evolved to metaphorically refer to 'coercion by crude means'.

A *cow-bell* is any large piece of hard metal protection, often hollow and indeed as bongy as a bell, designed to be placed in wide cracks. Whereas a *rurp* is a sliver of metal – a kind of piton (peg) intended to be gently hammer-tapped into very narrow incipient cracks. RURP stands for *realized unreality piton*. Phenomenologists the likes of Merleau-Ponty & Bachelard would have a field day!

A *pitch* is a section or a passage of climbing, it can be likened to a *leg* of a journey. A pitch is always shorter than a rope-length (which tends to range from 40 to 60m), but it is more often determined by the intricacies of the line, and distances between available ledges on which to make an anchor.

A *topo*, in this case, is a graphical representation of a crag & its climbs. This representation might be a photograph overlaid with bright lines that pick out the climbs, or might be a simple, even scruffy, hand-drawn sketch. *Topo* is presumably a contraction of *topographic*. (The author *is* aware that presumption can cause a traveller to believe the *lie of the land*.)

Climbers make use of a series of standard calls whilst climbing. The signal *Take in!* means that the belayar [see note below] should take in the slack rope. It is notable that the author in this piece has refused to use the signal call *That's me!* (which is usually shouted by the climber to the belayer to indicate that rope tautness or slackness is as the climber would like). Both Freud <u>and</u> Jung would have a field day with this!

Slackline & Tarn: There is of course no *Tagonachi Gap* in Japan, which makes it doubly a 'gap' !

The author's (or is it Nark's?) way of using the Japanese honorific address ~*san* is possibly incorrect, and is therefore potentially an affectation. At first the author wanted to be certain that it was correct, but came to realise that such potentially affected constructedness is *appropriate* to the fiction. The author is painfully aware that the word *appropriate,* if not reflected in, is certainly refracted through the word *appropriation.*

Cracked Gabbro: *Gabbro* is a very rough rock, rougher than even gritstone! Most of the Black Cuillin on the Isle of Skye are made of gabbro.

So you run and you run [...] is from *The Dark Side of The Moon* by Pink Floyd.

Smiles Balanced on Teeth mentions King Solomon & the Ark of the Covenant. The Ethiopian Orthodox Tewahedo (Christian) Church claims to possess the Ark of the Covenant, in Axum, Northern Ethiopia. Apparently, the Ethiopian Empire was established in 1270 as a Solomonic dynasty.

Be soft in the breeze, for strength is hardness – and hardness is a partner of death. This draws from the prayer in Tarkovsky's *Stalker: When a tree is growing, it's tender and pliant. But when it's dry and hard, it dies. Hardness and strength are death's companions. Pliancy and weakness are expressions of the freshness of being.*

The Ewe Stone: *Weather is the medium through which the mountaineer moves.* The author is unable to attribute this expression, but he first heard it at Outward Bound Eskdale in the English Lake District, whilst attending a Mountain Leader Training Board Summer Mountain Leader course, mid to late 90s. The phrase was uttered by a visiting speaker, who gave a lecture on outdoor clothing & technical fabrics.

Broad Stand, in the English Lake District, is a short rockface that bars the way between Scafell Pikes & Scafell. It is situated at the south-west end of the two mountains' adjoining ridge, at the col of Mickledore. Coleridge has famously recounted the descent that he made in August 1802. It is extremely unlikely that anyone had been that way, either in ascent or descent, before Coleridge. Some consider this a moment of pure, innocent, genuine adventure, and as being one of the earliest of mountaineering rock-climbing exploits. And some do not!

He now wanted nothing more than to get away as quickly as possibel. [sic] This is quoted accurately from the 1989 reprint of a famous poetry/fiction/drama collection first published by Faber & Faber in 1967. Hints are found elsewhere ... the potential, the possibility ... for transformation, be that garbled, or beautiful ... a middle-aged man's fear of poetics whilst at the same time his desire for it ... or rather his need ... this apparently prosaic line about wanting to get away ... 'get', as in to acquire, and 'away' that could so easily be typo-ed as: 'a way' ... this apparently prosaic line with its reference to 'nothing' & 'more' (these words abutting against or leaning into each other) ... and the adverbially camouflaged word 'quick' ... *a living thing ... the tender or sensitive flesh in part of the body ... living semblance ...* that line, that sentence with its correct grammar ... it ends with that misspelled word — 'possibel' — this is where the prosaic surface 'code' breaks ... open ... perhaps only a slight crack in the rock, but that is all the hydrogen bonds of Poetry's frost crystals need for leverage before all ... goes awry, or perhaps just goes ... else where ... for in poetics what is 'possibel', not what is certain, is the driver ...

The name – *Mount McKinley* – is a colonial superimposition upon the aboriginal name *Denali*. Denali is in what is now called Alaska, and it is the highest mountain on the continent of Turtle Island (now called North America).

Impossibly hard wall : Here – at least on the surface! – the word *hard* simply refers to how hard – as in difficult – the wall is to climb. *Hard* is a word often used in guidebooks to describe climbing that is actually especially hard. (Understatement & irony are common in British guidebooks.)

a 'Johnny Dawes' is a dot: Johnny Dawes is often described as *a legend of British climbing*. During the 1980s he produced the first rock-climbs to be graded E8 & E9 (the E standing for *extreme*).

Dawes is an artist of sorts – a unique visionary & practitioner of movement-&-adhesion. He is also a profoundly gifted poetic climber-writer. The poem focuses on Dawes' perception of friction as experienced on gritstone.

metal on: *krab* is a compression of *karabiner*.

Climber & Pedlar: The quoted verse has been attributed to Irvine Hunt – via the author's memory. The verse was taken from a laminated photocopied poem found in a Keswick cafe called The Lakeland Pedlar (early 21st Century). The author has failed to confirm this attribution via print or online.

The Bludgeon (which is not a *sandbag*!) is the name of a classic rock-climb on Shepherd's Crag in Borrowdale, in the English Lake District. The climb is not very hard by today's 'Kung-fu' standards, but at E1 far beyond the scope of nearly all climbers in 1907. E1 is still out of reach for the majority of leisure climbers, and in the wet The Bludgeon would be if not impossible, then a desperate undertaking for a modern climber. There are various outdoor brands & products mentioned in this poem. A *friend*, manufactured by *Wild Country*, is a metal-alloy camming device used for protecting a climb. *Edelrid* was the first company to manufacture modern, stretchy kernmantle ropes, which superseded the old hawser-laid types.

A *belayer* is the second who guards the lead climber by holding their rope(s), although *belayer* can also refer to a leader *bringing up their second*. Often a climbing pair will alternate their roles as leader or second, as they ascend a cliff. A belay-device – a friction-plate – is used to arrest the rope's running should the climber fall.

Crow Stone: Regarding the provenance of the image on page 116, in correspondence with Mark Goodwin on 12th March 2013, Jim Perrin replied: *Isn't it just fab! And playful! I've a vague notion it came from Mrs. Pamela Monkhouse – dear old Paddy's widow – years and years ago. Maybe credit "the late Pamela Monkhouse" and caption it "a Rucksack Club party at the Crowstones, c. 1926."*

In Slate's Hands: The Dinorwig Quarries in Snowdonia are of genuinely awesome proportions. For climbers they have become a slate-wonder-land. Quarrying began in the 1780s and finally ended in 1969. Much profit was extracted by Englishmen whilst Welsh quarrymen suffered appallingly.

Rainbow: There is an especially beautiful expanse of slate in the Dinorwig Quarries called the Rainbow Slab, thus named because of the bow-shaped strata-ripple running across it.

The Purest: *Once having learned to climb, the gods' godliest trick was giving up.* Attributed to Donnie Jaws by Tilly Billman during a conversation with Krama Woodgin.

Line is another word for *route* or *rock-climb*. Guidebooks will often refer to *a good natural line* when a climb follows an aesthetic-logic laid down by geology (or at least we can imagine it that way!). Sometimes a guidebook will describe a climb as having *a poor line*.

A *re-entrant* is a very small valley, or a gulley or inlet. A re-entrant is shown on a contour line as a V- or U- shape (pointing into the hillside).

That distant cache [...] refers to the South Col on the way up to Everest's summit, which – shamefully – is now essentially a garbage dump & cemetery for the unburied.

Craig was indeed born out of rock ... but Craig was also born out of a Crow born out of a poet ... thus The Cycle revolves ...

Crux refers to the hardest and therefore most crucial part of a climb. A climb's *technical crux* is at the most difficult move or sequence of moves. A *psychological crux* (if a climb has one) refers to a part of a climb, that whilst not being the most technically difficult, is by far the most frightening.

Gogarth is a rather tall and somewhat intimidating giant made of steep & crozzled quartzite. They, for the gender of Gogarth remains a mystery, dwell on the coast of Holyhead, Anglesey. In fact geologists would claim that they (Gogarth, that is!) *are* the coast of Holyhead, or at least a huge portion of it. Whatever their beliefs about science & myth, all climbers tend to treat Gogarth with very deep respect!

Solo means to climb without a rope, and thus the protection afforded by it. However, the solo-climber's intense focus can actually afford far more certain protection than the false sense of security sometimes imagined through ill-considered use of a rope.

Sheffield is a world-class centre of rock-climbing development. Back in the 80s the habit of training in (somewhat filthy!) makeshift climbing gyms was, to a large extent, pioneered in Sheffield.

Keeping Balance: *The sheep know.* The wind funnelled Sylvia Plath's heat away whilst she was on Wuthering Heights. Pitiless weather is just as able to funnel away civilizations' words.

As I Cramponed Up One Morning: A *cornice* is a wave-crest-curl of icy snow that overhangs the top of a steep mountain face, or that decorates, with a meringue-ripple, the tops of snowy ridges. A cornice is formed by the wind. These snow-structures are dangerous, in that they are prone to collapse.

A *serac* is any of various unstable fang-like (or phallic!) ice-structures found on glaciers or steep mountain faces. Falling seracs are terrifying destroyers.

Chomolungma is the proper original Tibetan name of the mountain that colonials named *Everest*. The true name translates variously as: *Mother Goddess of The World* or *Goddess Mother of Mountains*. The Nepali name for the mountain – *Sagarmatha* – translates variously as: *Sky Head* or *Goddess of the Sky*.

The Abode of Snow translates back into the original Sanskrit as *Himalaya*.

Névé is a kind of compact snow formed by a freeze-melt cycle, and to some extent by wind. Such snow is an excellent substance to climb on, with crampons & axes … however, it is also a surface that is likely to dangerously shed fresh snow-fall.

The Tale of The Journey: *Heaven's Walls* refers to a climbing area in Lost World. Lost World is one of the huge Quarries of Dinorwig. The proper name given by climbers is *Heaven Walls*, however, the author has chosen to add the apostrophe-s.

The Quarryman is the name of a revolutionary rock-climb first put up by Johnny Dawes, back in the 80s. *Watford Gap* is the name of a large notch through which the Dinorwig Quarries' main right-of-way footpath passes. This notch is very close to The Quarryman. (The author dwells not very far from the actual Watford Gap (in the English Midlands), and once piloted his narrowboat-home through it ... apparently the author mentions this *only* in passing ...)

(Hydro O(h)m): There is an entire hydro-electric power station 'secreted' beneath the quarries, inside the mountain ... the hum of this power station pervades the quarries and at different intensities depending on the acoustic quality of the tunnels & galleries you find yourself in. In the bottom of Lost World there was, and perhaps still is, a strange *seam of sound* that one can walk through ... this is perhaps a standing wave of sound, or some other acoustic phenomenon, and possibly caused by the two parallel levels (*the wet level & the dry*) that tunnel into Lost World.

The little slate-built *shed* in the bottom of Lost World has since vanished under a massive rock-fall. It is truly sad that this once very beautiful frondy realm in the bottom of The Quarries has now been totally erased by a craze of slate-rubble. Such is loss ... and thus is the relentlessness of entropy ...

Ony draws his line on a slice of slate. The definition of the word 'line' is given above, further up this rockery. The mercurial Ony is grounding himself at this point. What he is doing here, is looking at the slate cliff and visualising how to climb it ... in fact he is beginning to work out how he might put up a fresh new route, so as to ascend Heaven's Walls. As Ony visualises and

        dances the moves
        in air

        fingertipping his
        forecasted crimps

        his body & limbs
        hieroglyphing his

relaxed tenses of
futures

he again

and now
pauses to pick

up a tile of
slate & then

delicately – and with his
tongue just protruding

from his mouth
-corner as if to

keep some

arcane word stuck
there on

the moment
of release –

Ony with a shard
of slate as

stylus draws
        (dawes)
onto his tile his
desired

moves and
progress of

shapes with
which to

make (and

open)

his imagined line

An End of An Affair: Apparently the author is very pleased that OS have now returned to representing crag features more clearly on their 1:25 000 maps. The crag ornamentation is not black, as it was before 2009, but neither is it nearly invisible dot-matrix grey-scale. It is now printed in an 'optimum grey', being clearly visible whilst at the same time not obscuring contour lines. The author likes to think that his strident complaints to OS during 2010 might've had something to do with their, as he puts it, *re-instating the bedrock!* The author *has* been gently informed by someone who loves him – and is able to live with him – that this is actually *very* unlikely.

Dear Ramblers: Comment made by Joanna Croston: *The repetition [...] reminds me of the conventional way of using map and compass, looking down, looking up, looking down (finding what you previously read), looking up again, confirming etc. etc.*

In relation to **About Fields** Joanna Croston expressed the following: *One thing I find fascinating about the UK is the place naming and how everything is named, every knoll, every hill, every small glen, it's intrinsically linked to the history of the island. In Canada we have so much landscape and wilderness, thousands and thousands of peaks remain unnamed, there aren't enough names perhaps!*

(M)a(p)sk: Joanna Croston commented: *I had to read this poem several times and only when I read it aloud did it resonate with **me**. Interesting that!* [*me* was underlined-&-emboldened by the author of the poem.]

Pacing bearings. The author is referring to the craft of taking a compass bearing from a landmark, but also the measuring of one's distance from that landmark as represented on the map, and then one's literally counting foot-falls to measure out that distance on the ground ... whilst walking the line of the compass bearing ... This is actually also described – to some degree – in *An End of An Affair*.

Brown-orange lines refers to the contours on an OS 1:25 000 map. These are usually drawn at 10 metre vertical intervals, sometimes 5, but of(f) course never at 9 metres! Nine is a number that often holds poets in thrall!

Black Crag Grey: The quotes throughout are from Gaston Bachelard's *The Poetics of Space* (Beacon Press, 1994) and Andrew Jordan's *Hegemonick* (Shearsman, 2012). The blurb on the back of *The Poetics of Space* goes thus: *Thirty years since its first publication in English, French philosopher Gaston Bachelard's* Poetics of Space *remains one of the most appealing and lyrical explorations of home.* The blurb on the back of *Hegemonick* is this: *Memory and rehearsal. The cognitive processes upon which we have learned to depend, they keep us in our context, which is where we are screwed. She said, "Use your imagination to set yourself free, be inspired to think the unthinkable." And I did. But there are so many things that contain us.*

A *triangulation pillar* (or trig point) is a kind of small altar – essential to the First Ritual of Triangles that generated the first *Ordnance Scriptures* (also known as the *Scrolls of Topography*, or sometimes the *Knoll Scrolls* (not to be confused with the apocryphal *The Book of Knolls & Ledges*)). These pillars are numerous, and positioned throughout the Bristle Isles, usually on hill-tops. For many summiteers these objects have become foci of reverence, and even worship. According to Trigpointing UK: *There are 6857 pillars listed in the T:UK database. Whilst most of them have fallen into disuse, about 233 of them are currently used in the Passive Station network.* Many of these four-foot-tall pillars are painted white, and so from a distance – and especially in mist – 'a trig' often takes on the form of a squat, white-robed, and hooded Druid monk.

[/] : Legend has it, that the author invented this cartographic symbol to show a poetical line-ending made by the author, that is not apparent on the ground of the original prose the author is quoting.

h[er] : The author has invented this cartographic symbol to denote an area where mapping is uncertain, and where a being might be inclined to pause, wisely, and utter *er* ... rather than *is!* (It appears that it is not entirely clear to the author if the author is actually a *myth*, *mythter*, or *mythis*.) The symbol also stands in for something missing from the original ground of the prose the author is quoting – perhaps missing in the original, or perhaps omitted through translation, or perhaps ignored by the author. It has not been confirmed, but the letter *h* used in this cartographic symbol probably stands for *hiatus*.

[**/her**] : The author invented this cartographic symbol to show where a hidden key to a certain gender may be cached, and where such gender distinction is NOT overt on the ground of the original prose the author is quoting.

[**&**] : This symbol is supposed. It is also supposed to denote the possibility of – or alternatively the complete loss of – a connection. This symbol goes beyond invention, or never reached it.

The following comment – relating to *Black Crag Grey* – was made by Joanna Croston: [...] *that* [...] *deliberate and playful crossing back and forth between tenses. It reminds me of how I often feel in Europe or in a sacred place in indigenous Canada, I feel intrinsically linked to the history I know resides there but can only observe in the present. Sometimes it makes me feel good because I feel part of that history (by being there in the present) or sometimes I want to distance myself from it, the emotional burden of indigenous sites of massacres for example, I can't really handle.*

Ordrey Nancy Surefey: This 'personification' probably says more about just how fictitious the author is, rather than how fictitious the author's fictitious characters are.

green rip // here here here [...]: The green dashed lines on OS 1:25s denote rights-of-way – they signify where you are legally allowed to tread. However, these signified rights-of-way (or should that be ways-of-right?) – as drawn on *the* map – often do not coincide with *the actual* foot-worn paths on *the* ground. If you don't know this fact about the mapping of Wales & Endglan ... when it is misty on a moor ... horizontally raining on a mountain ... or is power-cut black on wasteland ... then ... by gods (of all genders!) you can get yourself really real

ly   lo

Acknowledgements

Sylvia Plath's poem *Wuthering Heights* is quoted from, and also informs some parts of *Rock as Gloss*.

Ted Hughes' book *Wodwo* is referenced throughout *The Ewe Stone*, and strongly informs that fiction. *The Ewe Stone* especially converses with *The Rain Horse*.

Craig references directly Ted Hughes' cycle of poems *Crow: From the Life and Songs of the Crow*.

The original *Cracked Gabbro*, *Dear Ramblers* & *Black Crag Grey* pieces have been necessarily visually re-interpreted so as to fit the new ground & page-shapes of the book *Rock as Gloss*. This skilled & creative 're-laying' of these poems' layout-maps was carried out by Brian Lewis – who is therefore an essential co-maker of the re-formed poems, as they appear in the book.

I am grateful for the following commissions & awards that have all in some way contributed to my making *Rock as Gloss*:

East Midlands Arts Writers' Bursary 1996 – awarded to write poems about 1930s poet climber Menlove Edwards.

Society of Authors Eric Gregory Award 1998. My thanks to the 1998 panel of judges, especially the chair, Penelope Shuttle ... for compliments and encouragement regarding the poems *Craft* & *Rock Climbing for Novices* (*Craft* appears in my book *Steps* (Longbarrow Press 2014).).

Year of The Artist commission: poet-&-climber-in-residence for Leicestershire Residential Services, 2000 – 2001.

East Midlands Literature Development Officer Network commission to write a long poem – titled *Museum of The Stanage-ophone* – and perform that poem live as part of the 24-8 Writers' Project reading tour, 2003.

My thanks to the following, for their critical comments and/or encouragement relating to individual poems &/or fictions in this collection: Nick Bullock, David Caddy, Claire Carter, David Cooper, Deb Cooper, Rob Cooper, Malc Baxter, Tara Cunningham, Arthur Crossland, Johnny Dawes, Ed Douglas, Paul Evans, Sally Evans, Louis Goodwin, Niall Grimes, Jeremy Hilton, David Hope, Katie Ives, Chris Jones, Daithidh MacEochaidh, Robert Macfarlane, Chris Mitchell, Jonny Mitchell, Helen Mort, Simon Panton, Jim Perrin, Chris Poundwhite, Whitney Smith, Gordon Stainforth, David Stead, Harriet Tarlo, Julia Thornley, James Wheeler.

Thank you to Alison Fell, who decades ago, whilst tutoring me on an Arvon Foundation writing course, put me right, and set me on the right line ... towards *Craig* ...

Special thanks to Joanna Croston for her critical comments and encouragement relating to the entire MS (prior to the inclusion of the Rockery).

Thank you to Paul Evans for his fine drawn lines that adorn the surface of *Rock as Gloss*. Thank you to Emma Bolland for the soft vaporous trails of wavering stone, which she stretched gracefully across the back of the jacket's form.

Thank you to Brian Lewis – collaborator editor-artist extraordinaire. And also the bravest 'flat-landeer', 'night-jaunter', & 'foolish walker' I know.

My deep gratitude to Nikki,
my ever-trusted partner
on this strange climb of a life!